the goodness game

Small acts really do make a Big Difference!

Bryan

the goodness game

Make the World Better
and Feel Awesome
While Doing It

BRYAN DRISCOLL

the goodness game
© 2024 Bryan Driscoll
First Edition

All rights reserved. No part of this book may be reproduced, distributed, or transmitted in any form or by any means, including photocopying, recording, or other electronic or mechanical methods, without the prior written permission of the publisher, except in the case of brief quotations embodied in critical reviews and certain other noncommercial uses permitted by copyright law.

Paperback ISBN: 978-0-9841890-0-7

Hardback ISBN: 978-0-9841890-1-4

Ebook ISBN: 978-0-9841890-2-1

Published by Bryan Driscoll
Printed in the United States of America

Disclaimer

This book is intended for motivational and informational purposes only. The author and publisher are not responsible for any actions taken based on the content of this book. The information provided is not intended as professional advice, and readers are encouraged to seek their own professional guidance in matters of finance, health, or other areas. The author assumes no liability for any outcomes or decisions made by readers after reading this book.

Internet Addresses: While the author has made every effort to provide accurate internet addresses at the time of publication, neither the publisher nor the author assumes any responsibility for errors, or for changes that occur after publication.

good·ness
| \ˈgu̇d-nəs\
noun

the quality of being kind, caring, and morally good, expressed through small acts that positively impact others:

Her goodness shone through in her everyday efforts to help those around her.

game
| \ˈgām\
noun

a structured activity that encourages participants to engage in acts of kindness or positive behavior, often with specific goals or rewards:

The goodness game makes helping others fun and rewarding.

CONTENTS

Preface ix
My Story 1
The Game Begins 13
   The First Goodness Game 18
   The Response 25
   The Case for the Kindness Ripple Effect 29
Set-up for the goodness game 35
   What is the goodness game? 35
   #1 - Give Without Remembering 36
   #2 - Not Everyone Is Your Assignment 37
   #3 - Identify Your Helping Style 37
   #4 - Create Your Goodness Budget 37
   #5 - Keeping Score 38
   The Setup 38
Examples & Case Studies 43
   A Few Key Principles Before We Jump In 46
   Why Play the Game? 47
Rule #1: Give Without Remembering 51
   The Two Ways to Give 51
   A Few Examples 54
   Keep Your Eyes Open for Opportunities to Play the Game 55
Rule #2: Identify Your Helping Style 57
   What Kind of Helper am I? 57
   The Five Types of Helpers 59
   Helper's Heart Test 61
   The Energy Element 65
   Sometimes You Need To Accept Help 70

Rule #3: Not Everyone Is Your Assignment 71
    Accepting Help 72
    Don't Overstep 72
    Pitfalls to Avoid as You Play the Goodness Game 74
    Tricksters and Schemers 75

Rule #4: Create Your Goodness Budget 77
    Finance Burnout 79
    Time Burnout 80
    Energy Burnout 82

Rule #5: Keeping Score! 85
    Did you know? 86
    Your Scorecard 88
    The Goodness Journal 90

The Compound Effect or "The Kindness Ripple" 93
    Inspire Others 96
    The Inner Effect—Having Faith in Exponential Growth 100
    Win/Win 101

Just Do It! 105

Bibliography 109

About the Author 111

PREFACE

Throughout this book, you'll notice "the goodness game" always remains in lower case, even when used as a title, and even on the cover. This is intentional. The goodness game isn't about anything formal. It isn't about recognition or focusing on ourselves.

It's about helping others. Selflessly, anonymously (when you can, more on that later), and without any expectation of return. You're going to feel better, don't get me wrong, but that's not what it's about.

It's about humbly helping others. It's about doing good for the sake of doing good. It's about putting goodness out into the world because it's good to do so.

With that in mind, I've intentionally chosen to keep the goodness game in the lower case.

MY STORY

"ARE YOU OKAY?" SHE ASKED, leaning out of the open window of her car.

I wasn't—not even close—but who does that? Who stops their car and checks on a stranger on the side of the road?

Not many people, that's for sure, but that's exactly what some random lady said when she pulled up to me on the side of the road. This was over twenty-five years ago in Orlando, Florida, when I was barely eighteen. I was walking to the Greyhound station, hoping to sleep there overnight because I had nowhere else to go. Her one small act of stopping to check on me lit the spark that would eventually create the goodness game more than two decades later.

But wait. What *is* the goodness game?

Before we discuss the specifics of the goodness game, I should probably back up a bit and explain why I was on that road in Orlando in the first place.

I'll start at the beginning. It was the late 90s, I was eighteen years old, and I was pissed at my parents. Being young and stupid, I got the great idea to hit up the Greyhound station in Pittsburgh, Pennsylvania, and take the next bus that was leaving. I didn't tell my parents; I just left. They never had a chance to stop me.

And so, to Orlando, I went.

I wasn't exactly prepared. I'd packed my red-and-white duffle bag with a pair of pants, a few t-shirts, boxers, and some socks before heading out. I only had about $200 to my name, but I didn't care. I was running away. I was nervous and excited. I always liked doing new things, and I didn't often think about the consequences.

For example, I'm more likely to jump out of an airplane and figure out how to build the parachute on the way down. I'm not saying this is the right way; it's just how I did things, which is how I ended up on that bus to Orlando without any idea what I was really doing.

So, I shouldered my duffle bag, boarded the bus, and headed off. I'd never traveled by bus in the past. If you've never done it, it's an experience. It's the cheapest way to travel; there are no bells or whistles. Plus, you meet some interesting characters. If I were going to run from the law, that's how I'd do it for sure.

I learned a few things quickly, such as not to sit in the rear of the bus next to the bathroom. I also had to learn how to make connections on the fly. With buses, it's not a direct ride. You have to stop and take connections the entire way to your destination. This means you're switching buses frequently, especially for such a long ride. The trip took about twenty-four hours, and I met some real characters on the ride.

One couple turned out to be the nicest people. They were on the last bus before I reached Orlando. It'd been one of the longest stretches, and everyone felt a little hyped up because we were finally getting off. I started making small talk with this couple. They asked where I was staying, and I told them I didn't know yet. I was going to figure that out when I got there. Keep in mind, it was about 11:00 p.m., and this was the 90s; I didn't have a cell phone, Uber didn't exist, and information wasn't as easily available as it is today. "Winging it" in the 90s was a completely different concept than it is today! I had *no idea* what I was going to do.

I'd never even *been* to Orlando!

The couple said they would help me find a hotel and took me to their place to call a few. I remember standing at their kitchen table with the Yellow Pages—and I'm sure you know what the Yellow Pages are—calling motels to see who had availability. We found a Days Inn that was cheap. I don't remember the exact price, but it was about $25 per night. Right in my budget!

They gave me a ride to the hotel, and that's where the story begins…I was out in the world and on my own.

Money runs out fast when you only have $200 and your motel costs $25 per night. My daily budget was about $30, so around midday when I couldn't stave off the hunger pangs anymore, I'd eat a Wendy's hamburger. Then, if I wanted to stick to my budget, I was pretty much on my own for entertainment and out of luck for dining. Not the most glamorous trip. It wasn't exactly what I had imagined when I lost my temper and decided to run away.

Though, to be fair, I hadn't really imagined anything. Remember? I jump, then figure out the parachute.

After about a week, I was running out of money and needed to come up with a plan. I went to apply for a job at a local grocery store. I walked in, asked for an application, and started to fill it out, then paused when I read the tiny letters under the blank line where I was supposed to write my address.

I thought, "I don't have an address. What am I going to do here?"

My next step was to ask to speak with the manager and see if I could "sell myself" into a job. I was eventually greeted by a nice guy in the produce department. We started talking, and I explained my situation and told him, "I'm looking for a job, and I'm hard working."

The manager was compassionate about my situation but explained the store was a corporation and had processes they were required to follow. To make matters worse, he also told me they paid bi-weekly, so my first check—*if* he could even get me hired—wouldn't be for weeks.

I needed to pay for my room now, so that wouldn't work.

"So now what am I supposed to do?" I remember thinking. "I have more problems than I thought—and I thought I had a lot of problems!"

I'd never even considered there would be issues with not having a phone number or address, much less that I might not get paid for weeks once I did find a job. I began thinking… hard. I needed a solution. Then I started on one of the toughest physical and mental journeys of my life.

I became a day laborer.

The term "day labor" is usually used to describe unskilled, nonpermanent labor that results in a paycheck of some sort (usually cash) at the close of the workday. The good thing about day labor is that you get paid each day. The bad thing is there's no guarantee you'll be getting more work tomorrow. You just show up and hope for work. Even then, we'd only get paid about $25 for the day. Granted, it was the late 90s, so the money went a little farther than it would now. At that rate, I'd barely break even after I paid for my room, but at least it was a start.

I showed up bright and early each morning to get my name on the list. With my name locked in, all I had to do was wait until someone pulled up—normally in a truck—looking for labor for the day. We'd all stand in a group, and the guy looking to hire someone would say something like, "I need ten guys to fix a roof." Then, you'd all stand there while he decided if you were one of the ten guys who looked like they'd be good for the job. There were women, of course. I only say "guys" because most of us were men.

As I stood in the clustered group of people with the hot Florida sun beating down on me, all I remember thinking was, "I hope I get picked." I watched as a guy looked us over. Looking back, it was a little weird to just stand there and be inspected, but at the time, I just hoped I looked like I was up for the job.

"I'll take you," the man said on my first day, though he'd been pointing at a guy in the front. Without a pause, my hopefully-soon-to-be-temporary-employer continued, "I'll take you," he said to a guy to my side, "and I'll take you." he finished, this time pointing at me. I was in! A cool quarter of a hundred dollars and another night with a roof over my head—but no hamburgers—were about to be mine.

I was pumped. I had no idea where we were going or what we'd be doing, but I had a job for the day. I was on board to do whatever needed doing.

We drove to the worksite, and it turned out we'd be working on an amusement park still under construction. I carried scaffolding from the job site across a parking lot. All day. For eight hours.

I remember they were building a huge tree, and our job was carting the scaffolding around. It was a long walk. Looking back, I'm pretty sure I was working on what would eventually become Disney's Animal Kingdom.

The day was hot—really hot—and I didn't pack lunch or have a water bottle. I didn't plan anything. Remember? No parachute?

Still, I toughed it out and did the work for a few days, but when you're broke and your room costs as much as you make in a day and there's no room in your budget for food…well, then you have a problem. People need to eat and drink to survive, and I wasn't currently on a path to survive unless I made some changes.

I had a serious problem that I needed to deal with as soon as possible. My solution was to save some money by doing away with my accommodation expenses. I checked out of the motel to increase my food budget. With nowhere to sleep, I started the walk to the Greyhound station and planned to sleep there for the night.

I never said it was a good solution.

I clearly wasn't thinking with any sense of my future. I was reacting to my circumstances, self-inflicted as those circumstances were. Panic had set in, and I didn't have any control over my situation anymore. I was just trying to survive. So I packed up my things, put them in my duffle bag, and started walking.

I remember how hot and humid the walk was as I passed through a pretty rough neighborhood on the way to the Greyhound station. My thoughts were racing, and each thought was cyclical and frightening. If the bus station noticed I was sleeping there, would they kick me out? They'd have to realize I didn't have a ticket eventually. Then, when they kicked me out, where would I sleep? I wouldn't be able to do this forever. I needed steady work. I needed meals. I needed a place to stay. This wasn't sustainable.

My mind kept racing, and the panic got worse.

I was about to turn into one of the stories where I was homeless and begging for money on the street.

And then it happened…The lady with the crazy questions entered my life in a Geo Tracker with faded black paint and a soft top. She pulled up to the side of the road, rolled down her window, and stuck her head out. A waterfall of frizzy grey hair spilled over the edge of the open window as her eyes smiled at me.

"Are you okay?" she asked gravely. "Where are you going?"

I swallowed, a nervous lump in my throat. "I'm headed to the bus station."

Her eyes looked at me knowingly. In the passenger seat, I saw her adult son shift forward to get a look at me. "The bus station?" she repeated.

"Yes. I'm headed to the bus station to sleep."

She offered to take me back to her house, where she lived with her son and husband. "I'll help you out," she said.

I don't even remember getting in, but I remember sitting in the back of that Geo Tracker, not yet knowing how lucky I'd just gotten. Of course, I know now.

So, about fifty minutes later, we pulled up to her house. It was a ranch house with a white picket fence, and the first thing I saw was a horse just kind of hanging out behind the fence. At the time, I thought this was odd. It wasn't a farm or anything;

it was just a house with a yard, and in the yard was a horse. No big deal.

It was a pretty simple one-story house. Probably built in the 60s, with a kitchen on the left, a living room on the right, and a dining table squarely in front of you. A quick walk around the table and through the dining room took you to a hall where the bedrooms were. My new bedroom was on the right.

That's right. I said *my* bedroom. It wasn't mine for more than a few nights, but it was mine. It was a room, indoors, and it had a bed, even if I did have to share it with the cat.

When we walked inside, the lady introduced me to her husband. They agreed they would let me stay the night. I stayed in "the cat's room." Yes, that's what they called it. It had a mattress on the floor for—you guessed it—the cat. This was no ordinary cat. He was about two feet tall and looked like a cheetah. I wondered if I'd have to fight him for the mattress, but it turned out okay in the end. What was even weirder is that I'm allergic to cats, but it was not a huge deal at the time. I was just a little stuffy—and, you know, *afraid*.

Thinking back, I have to ask myself, "Who picks up some ratty kid, covered in filth from a day of carrying scaffolding, who had no home and therefore no shower, walking on the side of the road, and then takes them home?"

I had no idea why they were so nice to me even back then, and I wanted to pay them back somehow. Then I ended up farther in their debt as they fed me dinner. A *real* dinner. Not homemade, but not Wendy's, either. We had spaghetti in canned sauce, and they let me eat as much as I wanted. I could feel the favor I owed this lady getting bigger.

I remember sitting at the table, talking with them as I scarfed down this spaghetti so fast. My stomach had been rumbling with hunger, and that spaghetti tasted so good. But even after my hunger was satisfied, I still felt a shadow of discomfort. I knew why: I don't like owing people favors, and I owed them a big one. I asked if the couple had something I could do for them around the house, but they didn't have anything. Even though my stomach was getting far more comfortable, I was getting progressively less so as I struggled to find a way to help out. I kept asking. Finally, the lady told me I could go outside and clean the grill for her. I breathed a sigh of relief.

However, when I got outside and looked at the grill, my discomfort returned. It took about five minutes to wipe it down because it was nearly spotless already. They hadn't needed the grill cleaned; she was trying to appease me so I'd stop asking what I could do to help.

You know the crazy thing? I can still remember their house. I can see it clear as day: their grill I'd cleaned in the yard, their enormous cat I definitely didn't cuddle with, and even their kitchen. But I can't picture them. This man and woman sheltered and fed me, and I can't recall either of their names. I want to say her husband's name *might* have been John, so we'll go with that.

Either way, he worked in the hotel industry, and after a day or so of staying at their house, they booked me a room at a Comfort Inn and helped me get a job at a different hotel that John worked at. This was a step up from the $25 per night hotel I stayed in just a week earlier. The deal was – they'd pay for the hotel stay—$300—and I agreed to pay them back with my first paycheck.

So, by this time, I'd been in Florida for a few weeks; my mom had no clue where I was, and I knew she was undoubtedly anxious and worried. Going AWOL had certainly been a jerk move on my part. It was awful just leaving and not telling anyone where I was going. Being a father now, I realize it must have been horrifying not knowing where I was. After about two weeks, I eventually reached out to my mom to let her know I was alive.

It might have been on that first call or a later one, but she told me there was a hurricane in South Florida, where my uncle lived. He needed help boarding up his house and was, coincidentally, coming to Orlando to drop off his wife in a hotel before driving back to Pompano Beach to prepare for the storm. It was pretty obvious where she wanted me to go.

I had to make a decision: Should I stay with the new job—I was still in training—or bail out and leave?

Before I tell you what I decided, I need you to understand a little bit about how I viewed work at that time in my life. I'd worked roughly twenty jobs by that time—quite a lot for an eighteen-year-old. The problem was I kept getting bored, and fast—you have to change jobs often to have twenty of them by the time you're eighteen. I worked at a hardware store, did sales, was a waiter, tried telemarketing, sweated it out in construction, and even took a shot at delivering pizza.

As you can imagine, bailing out on a job wasn't new for me, and yes, I bailed on the hotel job, too. I met up with my uncle and headed for Pompano Beach to help, leaving that lovely couple, the $300 debt, and the job opportunity they had helped get me, behind. I acknowledged my debt to them, but, in the end, after I helped my uncle, I made amends with my parents and went home to them. I didn't even think about that debt after a while. I had no money anyway, and I just went on with life.

A while later—still living with my parents—I ended up getting a job at the local cable company. I started to make some money and finally remembered what the lady in Florida did for me. I wanted to pay her back, but life kept getting in the way (lame excuse, I know). I'd think about it, but then remember I didn't have her contact info and forget about it again, or I'd decide I'd rather go out with my buddies and blow the money at the bar instead of paying off a debt that clearly no one was going to try to collect.

Basically, I was young, stupid, and living in the moment.

Eventually, though, the moment caught up to me. The feeling that I needed to repay the lady and her husband in Florida grew as I got older. I even asked my mom if she'd kept the address, but she also didn't have any way to contact the lady. Despite this feeling of an unpaid debt, there seemed to be nothing I could do about it.

I kept thinking back on the experience and realizing how strange it was. What are the odds that someone would pick up a stranger and help the way she did? Finally seeing this from her point of view was huge. This realization was a life-changing moment for me, and I didn't even realize what was happening at the time.

If she hadn't done that single, simple, kind deed, I'd have been sleeping on the street, and who knows where that would have ended. Likely, it wouldn't have ended well.

The only thing I can think of is that she was an angel. Not like an angel with wings from Heaven or anything like that, but she was an angel in the sense that she—for reasons I'll never know—decided to pull over on the side of the road and help me. I can only thank God for her, and it kills me that I *still* don't know her name or contact information.

If you're reading this, "John's" wife, please reach out. I owe you more than $300.

I'm telling you this story because it started my journey of consciously creating small acts of kindness. It changed the way I think about helping others. Looking back, this is where the goodness game all started.

THE GAME BEGINS

DURING THIS TIME, I WATCHED the movie *Pay It Forward* and got an idea. If you haven't seen *Pay It Forward*, the idea is that you help someone, and instead of them paying you back, they "pay it forward" to three people. This creates a compound effect. It's a fictional movie, but I wondered if this would work in the real world.

I remember it vividly; in April 2009—more than a decade after my incident in Florida—I was lying in bed around 10:00 p.m. and couldn't sleep. I had this idea, a really crazy idea, but I wanted to see what would happen:

I'd pick a random city and post something on Craigslist in the "Free Section," telling people I'd come to their city and help them. In exchange, I'd like them to pay it forward.

Picture this…I'm lying in bed and staring at the white ceiling with my heart racing. You know, one of those nights that you just can't sleep. Ideas just started pouring into my head. I could see it, play-by-play, exactly how I'd do it.

My mind was going a mile a minute. Energy poured in like a waterfall, and I jumped out of bed. I heard my heartbeat thudding in my chest. I could practically taste the adrenaline pumping through my veins.

I walked into the computer room—yes, I had a computer room—and it was dark. I didn't bother to turn on the lights and just sat down in front of the monitor. My eyes squinted for a minute until they adjusted to the bright screen.

I opened a map of the USA on my computer and grabbed my mouse. I closed my eyes, started moving the mouse randomly for about seven seconds, and listened as it scraped back and forth on my desktop. I stopped…and opened my eyes.

I scanned the screen to see where the cursor stopped, and the white arrow was sitting directly atop Chicago.

My excitement grew. I exhaled heavily. Relief. Step 1 was now complete.

I created a post on Craigslist, and here's what it said:

> "I know this may sound a little crazy, but bear with me.
>
> What I would like to do this weekend is help a few people that need help. I only have Saturday and Sunday to do this, so I will try my best to do what I can. I don't have much $$$, but I am willing to give my time, etc.
>
> All that I ask in return is that you Pay It Forward.
>
> If you haven't heard that saying before, what that is, is that I don't want anything in return. I just want you to help someone in the future someday, if you can.
>
> So I am willing to do pretty much anything (almost anything). I can help you with groceries, give you a ride if you need one, help around the house/yard, or shoot me an email, and I'll let you know if it's something I can do.

I am going to try and do this in one city every month for the next year and see if any good comes from it. Maybe it will; if not, I'm sure it will leave some smiles and help some people out.

If you think it's a crazy idea, please keep the thoughts to yourself."

Emails started flooding in. I thought I'd get a ton of emails with really big things—you know, the big lift types of things.

Here are a few of the emails I received (I left the typos for authenticity):

"I saw your ad on craigslist. You are a wonderful person. I am feeling down in life right now, but when I read your ad, I felt better just knowing that good people are still around! I always have things to be grateful for. God bless you."

"Hey - great to see someone else contributing to society. I posted something like this many months ago and kept getting flagged. Ended up helping someone put together a bunk bed for her kids (single parent) and fixed her dishwasher. You will be blessed for doing this kind of work.

Shoot me an email if you need some help brother
God Bless
Paul"

> *Now I am going to try to figure out a way to do the same. Thanks for the inspiration.*
> *Gaby"*

> *"Thanks, if you need some help, let me know. Pretty well skilled, fortunately I'm fine financially (I've always worked hard, enjoy working, and don't spend) Best of luck to you, we can all make a difference with a little effort.*
> *Rick"*

> *"dude, this is the craziest...idea i have ever heard...i truly wish you the best and damn if i could tag along...i would love if you would keep me updated and hell if your in my area...i will help out with what i can...it really does feel good to help from the heart, and im right there with you in spirit...*
> *cindi"*

And then I started to get a few emails that I could actually help with (same with the typos)...

> *"Hi how would you like to help me take apart a swing set on Sunday? Please let me know*
> *Mandy"*

"Laid off worker doing side jobs to stay afloat. Need a battery for my van, used-old-loaner-new. Mines is dead. Need van to continue doing side jobs. If you can do anything it would really help. Thank you and God bless
Angel"

"Hi, my name is Mike…Great message you are sending! If only more people heard that message…I rarely ask for help, but tomorrow (Saturday) I need to pick up a used truck that I just bought.

The trouble is,, I live in Des Plaines and the truck is about 45 min away, in Oak Lawn. I just need a ride there…If you can fit me in, (I understand more "needy" requests should take priority over mine), shoot me an email or call me at 847-xxx-xxxx…

Thanks,
Mike"

So, I looked at this like it was a sign, and off I went.

The First Goodness Game

My mission was to:
- Help Mike pick up his car
- Get a car battery for Angel's car—I'd need to purchase this
- Help Mandy move a swing set
- Help Demo a Bathroom
- Drop Clothes at the homeless shelter

I grabbed some clothes, including a Pittsburgh Steelers AFC Championship Sweatshirt, a pair of black and white Jordans, and a National Wildlife Turkey Federation hat, and some tools, and I was off.

The Game Begins

I was pretty nervous but also really excited. I was going to meet strangers off the internet—exactly what you're told not to do when you're younger. I prayed I wasn't meeting any people with ill intentions, just as they were probably praying *I* didn't have ill intentions.

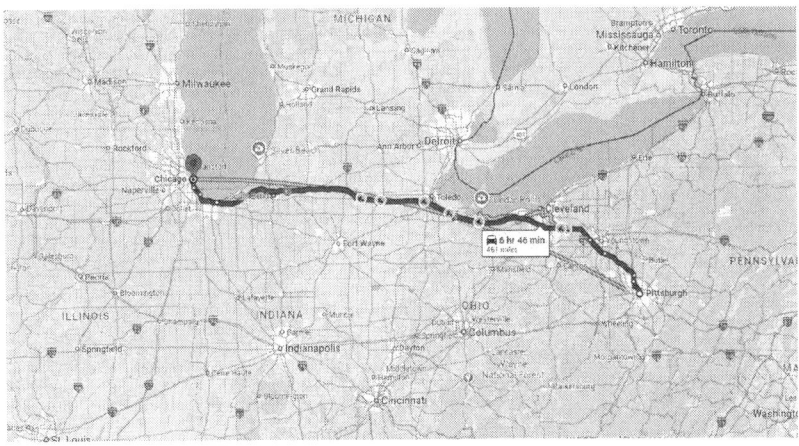

I had an old-school camcorder with me—this was before the time of smartphones that took videos. I brought this to document the trip, although I wasn't sure what I'd do with it yet. To start, I just recorded random parts of the trip, including the part where I was driving down the highway listening to Lady Gaga. I was taking a leap of faith and seeing where it went.

It was about an eight-hour drive, and I finally pulled into my hotel. I drove straight through, so it was nice to relax before the activities started in the morning.

the goodness game

First off, I met Angel. He just needed a car battery. I met him at the store and picked up a Duralast battery. This was the only thing that I actually bought—every other act was paid for with "sweat."

Then, I went to meet Mike. He only needed a ride to pick up a new car he was buying. It was about forty-five minutes away. Again, this was before you could press a button on your phone, and a car would show up. I met him, we drove to his car, and he bought me a Chicago-style hot dog when we were done.

Next, I went to meet a guy who was actually helping someone else out with a bathroom remodel. He just needed help demoing it. I spent about four hours with him, helping him carry the debris outside. This one probably took the most effort. He already had all the walls pulled down, and the drywall and wood piled in the bathroom. We just needed to load it into garbage cans and drag it outside to the trash.

The Game Begins

Mandy was fourth on my list. Someone was giving her a swing set. She's the one I brought the tools for. The plan was to pull down the swing set and load it into a truck so they could take it back home for her kid.

And my last stop before leaving Chicago: the homeless shelter of a guy I talked with via email. Here, I dropped off the clothes. I remember going in, and they had rows of people making sandwiches. This organization meant business. I was happy I could help in the little way I'd been able to.

I left the homeless shelter and took the highway home. I remember driving back to Pittsburgh and being on such a high. The world looked brighter; my mood was humming, and I just felt lighter. It felt like I wanted to jump out of my body.

About halfway home, I realized two things:

1. I felt a deep sense of satisfaction, as if I'd just discovered my purpose.
2. I realized that I went out to help people, and I was the one who got the real benefit.

This took a while to sink in. When it did, I was hooked, and that's where the goodness game started, way back in 2009, though I didn't realize I was playing a game then. As soon as I got home, I pulled out my laptop and opened Microsoft Movie Maker. I'd never made anything online before. I pulled my images into Movie Maker, did a voiceover, and created a video showing the trip. It was nothing fancy, but it did a good job telling the story.
If you're interested, you can watch the video at www.goodnessgame.com

The Response

I posted the video on YouTube, and that was that...or that's what I thought until a day or so later when it started to get comments. Before long, they started pouring in.

Comments like this (again, I left the typos for authenticity):

> "friendinpittsburgh made my day.
> The more we can embrace this attitude- the better we'll all be.
>
> We're all in this life together and we're all effected by those around us- let's continue to make this a better life for our neighbors... And friends we don't yet know we have."
>
> "I saw this ad on Craigslist in Chicago and immediately emailed to find out what the motivation was for such a kind act. I was so blessed to find out that this real like [life] "pay it forward" came without ulterior motive and simply came from a servants heart. I have been truly blessed by this story. THANK YOU!"

And then I got this!

> "Hello,
> I am a freelance reporter for the Windy Citizen in Chicago and after watching your video and reading all

the amazing comments, I am very intrigued by your story. I would love to chat more with you about your experiences and the people you met along the way. The concept of "paying it forward" is really inspirational and I would love to hear more about it.

I hope to hear from you soon,
Gabrielle"

I was thinking, "This is awesome!" But I was also conflicted. This wasn't about me—this was about inspiring others to help each other. It was about showing them that small things make a big difference.

A few other reporters also hit me up, asking to do interviews.

Ultimately, I decided to do the interviews on one condition: they had to leave my name out. Most said they couldn't do the story because they needed a name in the story to make it work. They said it's hard to do a story without a person in it.

I needed them to leave my name out of the story because I believed that if I put a person behind this act, then people would relate differently. They might say things like, "Well, he can do that because he's twenty-nine and doesn't have a family," or "he can do it because he lives at home," or, well…whatever reason. You get it.

My theory was that if I didn't put a name or face behind the story, people could imagine themselves being able to do it as well, and it would have a bigger impact. By the way, this turned out to not always be true, but we will talk more about that later.

Gabrielle said she'd have to talk with the editor—or whoever you talk with at the paper—and get back to me. She later came back and said they could do it. The *Windy Citizen* article referred to me as "The Steel City Samaritan" and highlighted the impact of small acts of kindness, saying, "Sometimes getting a little break isn't such a bad idea."

The article was published on April 14, 2009 (you can read it at www.goodnessgame.com), and spread like crazy. Platforms like CNBC, *Huffington Post*, and many others shared the piece. Other outlets became interested in what I was doing. One of those was *The Pittsburgh Post Gazette*.

When I talked with the *Pittsburgh Post Gazette*, their article hit the front page. Reporter, Michael Fuoco wrote, "In a virtual world filled with narcissism, rip-offs, and come-ons, the YouTube video '*Pay It Forward—Pittsburgh to Chicago*', feels like a visit to Mr. Rogers' neighborhood."

That article started an awesome chain reaction. I suddenly was hearing from people all over who were 'paying it forward' because my video had inspired them.

That's when I realized that something small could create a huge chain reaction of positive energy. One small act, driving to Chicago and helping a few people, reached thousands of others. It possibly brightened their day and maybe even inspired them to do something nice for someone else, too.

In my opinion, this publicity that was spreading my attempt to pay it forward proved that the model worked. I wanted to keep the momentum going. As in business, when we prove that a theory or idea has merit and can be successful, we say, "I can prove the model worked." That's what I'd done. This wasn't *just* an idea now. Sure, it had started as an idea. Then I took action—kind of like doing an experiment, though I didn't truly know what I was doing. The idea quickly became much, much more. What I hoped would happen with the "pay it forward" weekend turned out to be true. By taking an idea and matching it with positive energy and action, I was able to do something that had a life of its own.

As I worked through all of this in my head for the first time, I realized how big it had become. I'd just been lying in bed a few nights ago and had an idea to post on Craigslist. Now, national news outlets were writing about it and spreading the message! This was a big break for me. This external validation was the difference between thinking I was crazy and seeing something work in the "real world." At that point, I felt the model was proven. I'd started with a small act and got positive energy in front of hundreds of thousands of people using very little time and money.

Mission accomplished!

Or so I thought…

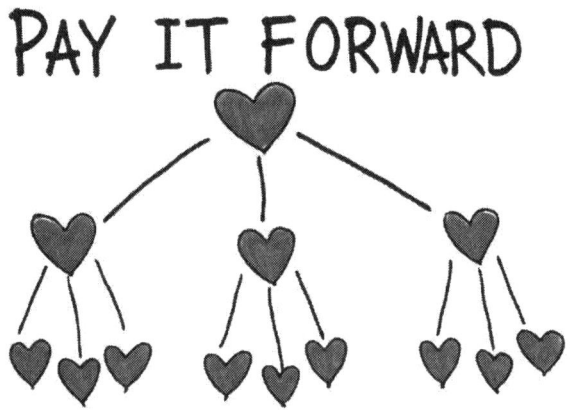

I'd struggle to maintain the momentum my mission required. I could pay it forward, but how could I magnify the effects? How could I make the biggest impact in the world around me and keep this thing going?

The Case for the Kindness Ripple Effect

I started doing some digging and found a lot of fascinating information. According to the 52 Lives Charity School of Kindness, kindness has a ripple effect. The organization states that we inspire others to be kind when we're kind (The Science of Kindness, 2022). Studies show that acts of kindness do, indeed, create a ripple effect that spreads outwards to our friends' friends' friends. That's an impressive three degrees of separation! This means that when you're kind to one person, that one act of kindness can positively affect up to 125 people!

Social scientists from UCLA's Bedari Kindness Institute have studied whether kindness is contagious. Their conclusion? Of course it is! An article in UCLA Magazine's Winter 2023 edition talked about one of these studies. The study concluded that simply as a result of witnessing a small act of kindness, others feel better about their neighborhood and community (Wolf 2023).

Through my model, I'd proven that small acts of kindness allow for the spread of *more* small acts of kindness, and so on. Now, I read that even university studies show that kindness can be contagious.

With my new insight, I returned to my original question: "How do I keep this going?"

To my surprise, an answer came: "Write a book!" So here it is. Welcome to your personal set of directions to the goodness game and my reason for writing the book.

Now that you know the history, in the next sections, I'll break down the things I learned over the past twenty-odd years of doing small acts of kindness. Then, I'll break down how I do it, the benefits I see in others' lives, and the benefits I see in my own life. My goal is to inspire you to help others and know that making a difference doesn't have to be something huge and grandiose. It's actually the small things that can make the biggest difference.

When I say small things, your "little act" can genuinely be very little. It could be opening the door for someone with a smile, letting someone merge into your lane instead of staying as close as you can to the bumper in front of you during rush hour, paying for someone's coffee behind you in the drive-through, helping a neighbor out when they need a hand, or maybe just listening to someone that's having a hard time and being there for them.

Seriously, super small stuff.

This game is 100% doable and 100% winnable! In addition, it creates a win/win situation because **you get to feel good**—you know, that whole karma thing. I've found that the more you help others, the better your life gets. You can do this by doing small things to help others, hence the goodness game.

Speaking of small acts—let me explain in more detail what I mean when I talk about "small acts having a large impact." Think back. At some point in your life story, there was almost certainly a small thing that changed the course of your life. That's what we're aiming for: small acts that leave a lasting impact.

Think about the story I told at the beginning of the book. How the lady picked me up on the side of the road. Ultimately, that was a huge act for me. It changed everything about where I was headed. For her, however, it may have been just a small act—though maybe picking up a stranger isn't *exactly* a small act. Either way, I quickly disappeared from her life. Literally. If they remember me at all, it's certainly only to wonder what happened. That dinner and ride were a small—maybe medium—act for her that made a huge difference in my life. That's just one example of how our actions can have big repercussions, *even if we never learn about them.*

To understand just how big those repercussions were, let me give you a little more background: As I mentioned earlier in the book, I never really looked at consequences like others did.

It's pretty obvious to me as I look back at my younger life now. If you haven't figured it out yet, I used to be a troublemaker. I failed at so many things in life. When I say "fail," I'm talking about things like:

- Almost dropping out of high school with a month or two left in my senior year (thanks, Mom, for making me stick it out)
- Getting in trouble with the law many times (mostly alcohol-related)
- Losing money at basically every business or financial endeavor I tried (I eventually figured this one out. I now own a marketing company with employees all over the world and invest in real estate)
- Spending some time in a mental ward (long story, but when you don't sleep for a few days, you break your brain)
- The list could go on and on

Life has punched me in the face so many times that I came up with the motto back in the late 90s: "Just try one more time." It was like everything in life I did, I failed. Some of those failures stung harder than others. However, the "pay it forward" Chicago trip was a win. That made a huge impression on me.

Now, being punched in the face by life has some benefits if you don't quit. You get tough and eventually figure things out. Case in point: I'm a husband, a real estate investor, a father to three amazing boys, and a business owner with over twenty employees.

I tell you this because I'm probably very similar to you. Maybe not in owning a business, maybe not in being a parent, and maybe not in our backgrounds, but we're the same because everyone deals with struggles, and everyone gets punched in the face. My exact situation might differ from yours, but everyone deals with these things. Regardless of our differences, one area I bet we're very similar is that at some point in your past, like in mine, someone has done a small act that has made a big difference in your life.

That commonality is why I decided to write this book. Anyone can make a difference through small acts of kindness and goodness, no matter their background or past. I've learned some things over the years that helped me tremendously. I want to share these things with you. If I can do it, anyone can do it. I feel it's my duty to pass this energy along and see what kind of impact we can make.

This isn't a "just be nice to others" type of book meant to be nothing but a feel-good read. This book aims to give you a roadmap to make a difference through small acts. I want to break things down to the simplest form, show you how to make a difference by doing one small act at a time, and prove to you it's easier than you think. This last thing is key and is worth repeating: it's easier than you think!

So, get ready to play the goodness game!

SET-UP FOR THE GOODNESS GAME

> **"AS LONG AS YOU ARE ALIVE, NEVER BELIEVE THE GAME IS OVER."**
>
> - IYANLA VANZANT, INSPIRATIONAL SPEAKER AND AUTHOR

What is the goodness game?

Now that you know a little bit about me, it's time for you to learn more about the goodness game. What is it? Essentially, the goodness game is a way to be intentionally kind. It's a way to deliberately put some goodness into the world. By turning it into a game—complete with a scorecard—we'll be more conscious of our actions and more likely to be the kind of people we want to be.

It's a game you can play by yourself, with friends, or even with strangers, and it's designed to help you help others and, by doing so, help yourself. I think most people try to help themselves by focusing on "self-help." However, I've found that the more you focus on helping others, the more you end up helping yourself.

So, let's start the same way we would if we were learning any classic board game: dive right in without reading the instructions and then get annoyed with our family and friends.

Just kidding. Let's start with a brief overview of the rules. Then we'll get into the nitty-gritty of how to play this game.

#1 - Give Without Remembering

The way I see it, there are two ways to give: Either the recipient knows who you are, or no one knows. We'll discuss an exception in the next chapter, but for now, keep these two in mind. There are times when one of these options is more appropriate than the other. Sometimes, the recipient *has* to know. Part of learning the rules of the goodness game is identifying which option is the best in a given situation.

#2 - Not Everyone Is Your Assignment

We can't help everyone. Indeed, we *shouldn't* help everyone. Not everyone is meant to be our assignment. I'm not qualified to help with a drug problem. Offering direct help might actually be counterproductive. My job would be to point the person toward whoever can help. *That's* how I help. It's now up to the next player in the goodness game, whether they realize they're playing or not.

#3 - Identify Your Helping Style

We'll give you the "helper type" test later in the book to see what type of helper you are. We'll also be doing an energy audit to determine what type of things you might gravitate toward and what type of things you might want to avoid.

#4 - Create Your Goodness Budget

Most people think about budgeting *only* with money, but with the goodness game, you'll need to budget your time, money, and energy. We'll go through the different budget strategies you can use so you're ready when you see an opportunity to help.

#5 - Keeping Score

The scorecard—more in that chapter—will allow you to see exactly how your mood and life are affected by playing the goodness game. We'll talk about how to win the game and we'll get into a little science showing why the game makes you feel so good.

THE SETUP

As with any good game, there's a bit of setup to handle now that we know the rules of the game. We'll need to identify our play style—yes, there are different ways to play—then we'll learn who we can play it with, and how long we should play.

MY PLAY STYLE

The good news is that you can play the goodness game however *you* want. We'll be running through some quizzes later in the book that will give you an idea of your ideal play style. This is the time to think about what kind of helper you are and choose which direction you'll take as you play the goodness game. Part of the game's "setup" involves figuring out what makes you tick. Ask yourself, "What gives me energy?"

For example, I hate cleaning my house. It *drains* my energy. On the other hand, some people love cleaning. They *gain* energy and enthusiasm when they finish giving the house a thorough once-over. Maybe it's knowing the house is clean or the satisfaction of accomplishing something. Either way, that's just one example of how certain activities can give or drain our energy.

Set-up for the goodness game

The same thing goes with your helping style.

Identifying and implementing the right helping style is crucial to your success in the goodness game.

So, ask yourself, "How do I like to help people?"

- Do you like to help people financially, spending little or no personal time helping? That's how I do it most of the time now that I've succeeded a bit more in my professional life.
- Do you like to be boots on the ground, maybe helping out at the soup kitchen or fixing someone's car?

It's important to figure out your helping style so you can do what you're built for and passionate about. To help with this, we'll go through a few short quizzes that will help you determine what type of helper you are. We'll really lay it out for you.

After you determine what type of helper you are, what your style is, and what your next step is—then it's time to act. Don't worry, we'll go through all the rules in the next chapter. For now, just know that the action steps are small and simple. It's about small acts making a big difference, so don't get held up on this last step. The goal is to start and take it small.

And, hey, this *is* a game! So, you'll also have a scorecard to track your results (more on that later). You'll be able to see a clear cause-and-effect pattern from playing the game.

Who Do I Play With?

Great question. Here are some ideas:

- You can play by yourself (and the world is who you play with). This does not have to be a team sport!
- Family—Your kids, spouse, parents, etc.
- Friends—From church, work, or anywhere
- Whoever you're dating—wouldn't it be a really interesting first date! Plus, you'd learn a lot about the person.
- Teachers
- Work associates—Your boss, co-workers, or even your employees
- Meetup groups—book clubs, church, homeschool groups
- Remote workers or social media friends—How awesome would it be to play the goodness game with someone from across the country?
- Masterminds or networking groups—I'm in a group that promotes one thing per event to try and make a difference.
- Parents of your kids' friends
- Even strangers
- So basically anyone…

Set-up for the goodness game

HOW LONG SHOULD I PLAY?

We'll break your gameplay into phases. I'm not a fan of huge commitments myself, and maybe you're not, either. The purpose of the phases is to test your experience with the goodness game, and, if you have a positive outcome, you proceed to the next phase.

> **Phase 1:** Seven Days: You start playing for the next seven days. At the end of seven days, you'll make the decision whether or not to move onto Phase 2.
>
> **Phase 2:** Once you see how awesome Phase 1 was, you're going to want to keep going. Phase 2 is thirty days. The key to this phase is to be consistent, but you don't have to play *every* day. Thirty days is quite a while, so stick with it!
>
> **Phase 3:** That's it; you're a player for life. According to James Clear, author of *Atomic Habits*, it takes about sixty-six days to form a new habit. At the start of Phase 3, you're more than halfway to making the goodness game a habit. Things will never be the same, and that's a good thing!
>
> **Bonus Phase:** Now it's time to add some players! You've hopefully been playing for at least a few weeks, hopefully longer. Why not pass *this* book along to a friend? Or, if you just can't part with it, get them their own copy.

Don't take my word for it. Try it out for seven days and see the effects for yourself. This is a never-ending game, and the more you play—the more you win! It's like eating healthily: the more you do it, the better you feel, and you'll want to keep doing it.

Of course, change isn't fun for a lot of people. Start small and be consistent. Uncomfortable things become comfortable pretty quickly if you do them consistently.

This might seem like a lot, but I'm not saying you have to help everyone every day. Remember, not everyone is your assignment. In later chapters, we'll get into how to manage your time, energy, and money to help you avoid burnout and continue making a positive difference in the world.

EXAMPLES & CASE STUDIES

Here are a few examples of playing the goodness game to get your wheels spinning.

EXAMPLE 1: RAINY DAY WIN/WIN

It was pouring outside. I'm talking about the kind of rain where you pull over on the side of the road because you can't see. I was going to the dollar store to grab something. I grabbed the few items I'd come for and was waiting in line to check out when I noticed a round container sitting there with about twenty umbrellas in it.

As I looked at them—the goodness game in mind—I knew I had to buy them all.

I rush back to my car, and as I'm getting drenched, I think, "I gotta do something here." I didn't know what, not yet, but I was in the zone. So, I called up my buddy Sean Martin—yes, I always call him by first and last name—and asked him if he wanted to go do something fun. I said I didn't know yet what that meant, but it involved umbrellas.
He said he was in, so I drove to his house and picked him up. We brainstormed for a few minutes and then drove to downtown Pittsburgh. It was getting dark by now, and the rain still hammered down. People were rushing about, trying to take

cover on their way to their car or bus. The rain didn't look like it was letting up anytime soon.

We drove around with twenty umbrellas in the back seat. I'd find a drenched pedestrian, and Sean Martin would hop out and give them an umbrella, usually without saying a word. Then we were off in search of the next person.

People were shocked. Who just pulls up and gives you an umbrella in the pouring rain? We probably looked a little suspicious, to be honest, which only made it funnier. It was like we were executing reverse pranks.

For me, I couldn't help but think about the lady who'd pulled up to me on the side of the road years earlier, in Orlando. The only difference was that it had been in broad daylight, and today, it was pouring rain. And we were giving umbrellas away instead of offering rides. And no one came home to eat with me. And we did it twenty times.

As we rushed from soaked pedestrian to soaked pedestrian, we didn't really get to sit and chat with the people to see what they thought once they realized they weren't being kidnapped, but you could see it in their eyes, some of them even offering a quick, "Thank you!"

This is one example of a small act of kindness that cost less than $20, connected with twenty strangers, and created a fun time for Sean Martin and me.

EXAMPLE 2: SMALL ACTS

A more recent story comes from Jennifer, who runs an organization in Pittsburgh called Harvest Street Mission. They connect people who are homeless with people who want to help serve food. Jennifer coordinates a group of people every week to make a huge amount of food, and then they go downtown and feed the homeless. Of course, that definitely exceeds the definition of "a small act," but in this big act, there are a lot of small opportunities. Jennifer once told me of a time when one of these small opportunities made a big difference.

She said: "One of our volunteers"—let's call him Fred—"makes it a priority to hand out new underwear every week. We have one guy who comes, and he's very large. It's hard to find his size. Last week, Fred gave the gentleman two pairs in his size. When Fred gave it to him, he used his first name, and the man thanked him for remembering his name. It wasn't *only* the underwear that mattered—though I'm sure it did—but that he knew his name. Small things matter!"

Who would have thought? The man was more grateful for someone remembering his name than the actual item given to him. This shows that something you consider small or trivial might be huge to someone else!

A Few Key Principles Before We Jump In

I know you're excited; I know I am! But, before we get into the rules, there are a few things to keep in mind as you finish reading and start playing:

- **It's important to take time to enjoy the ride.** I noticed in my life, I tend to focus on where I'm going instead of enjoying the moment. You'll want to make sure you enjoy yourself. Try to be present while you're playing the game.

- **Reflect and adapt so you learn from your experiences.** This is a new thing you're doing. You'll probably like some parts of it and hate others. That's okay. Adjust over time. The important thing is to start; we can always pivot when necessary.

- **Consistency is huge.** The things we'll be doing are going to be small, at least at first. This is to help stay consistent. You'll want to make helping others a habit.

- **Again, enjoy the ride.** This is worth repeating. Focus on the positive impact that you're making. Just as importantly, pay attention to the positive impact the game has in your life.

So, on to the game…

What? Still not convinced you should play? Let's talk about it for a minute.

Why Play the Game?

Playing the goodness game has no real downside, but there's a major upside. Why wouldn't you want to try something with no significant negative effects with the potential for all kinds of positive ones?

But what positive effects, you ask?

If making the world a better place isn't enough, here are a few *personal* benefits of playing the goodness game.

- **Motivation when you're feeling down:** I live in Pittsburgh. In the winter, the sun is barely out, and it's easy to get seasonal depression or seasonal affective disorder (SAD). In fact, *Psychology Today* reports that 10 million Americans suffer from SAD. Playing the game is often a great motivation to get out and about when you would otherwise spend a day inside.
- **Positive focus:** The game keeps your mind focused on things that are positive rather than negative self-talk.
- **Be yourself:** The game allows you to be yourself and do things that you're built for. Part of the game's purpose

is to help you discover what's natural for you, and then encourage you to go and do it!

- **Strengthen your relationships:** It helps strengthen the bonds with your spouse, kids, parents, and anybody else you play the game with.
- **Mental health:** The game keeps you in a positive mood and thinking proactively instead of constantly being hard on yourself. When you're helping others, it's difficult to be hard on yourself.
- **Compassion and empathy:** You have an opportunity to teach yourself and your kids—if you have them—how to be empathetic and compassionate.
- **Self-audit:** You'll discover your strengths and weaknesses while playing the game.
- **Leadership**: You'll learn how to lead better—if you choose to.
- **Connection:** You'll build stronger connections and make new friends by playing.
- **Inspiration**: You'll inspire others while motivating and inspiring yourself.
- **Spiritual:** Helping others gives you the chance to strengthen your connection with God.
- **New opportunities:** You'll become more at ease getting out of your comfort zone and being in new situations.
- **Be surprised:** Unexpected positive experiences will almost certainly come from your actions.

This is just a list of some ways you may benefit from playing the game. The list could go on and on, and I urge you to just take my word for it and play. The risk is low, and the reward will be high.

You picked up this book for a reason. Maybe you're looking for purpose, meaning, fulfillment, connection, or community. Maybe someone gifted you this book because it inspired them. Or, maybe you just want to do something—you want to *help*—and don't know where to start.

That's why I created this game. To make helping others easy and take away the guesswork. In the future pages, you're going to learn a few things about yourself, like what type of helper you are and what kinds of things give you energy and forward momentum.

Once you learn these things about yourself, you'll have a clear direction of what your next step is so you can start creating an impact, both in your life and the lives around you.

A final word on the instructions and getting started with the goodness game: **Don't overthink it.**

You only need to take the first step: Follow the process and see where the game takes you. New things can be scary, but I'm here to help you along the way. And don't worry! The best thing about this game is that you can't lose!

RULE #1:
GIVE WITHOUT REMEMBERING

> "ALWAYS GIVE WITHOUT REMEMBERING AND RECEIVE WITHOUT FORGETTING."
>
> – BRIAN TRACY, AUTHOR OF *EAT THAT FROG!* AND *EARN WHAT YOU'RE REALLY WORTH*

RULE #1 STATES,

"YOU MUST GIVE FREELY, ANONYMOUSLY (WHEN ABLE), AND WITHOUT EXPECTATION OF RETURN."

This rule is there to stop us from bragging about helping others. We don't broadcast our good deeds; we just do them. The way I see it, there are two ways to give without remembering.

The Two Ways to Give

#1 — YOU'RE THE ONLY ONE THAT KNOWS

I look at this as the purest form of giving. You're giving anonymously, and the recipient doesn't know who helped them. When you do this, you're literally giving without remembering as you don't get any recognition: no thanks, no nothing.

#2—YOU AND THE RECIPIENT KNOW

Sometimes, you can't help out anonymously. You *have* to do it so the recipient knows. This is still a great way to give! After all, everyone saw Sean Martin's face when he passed out the umbrellas. With this way of giving, you help someone out and they accept the help. That's the end of it. There's no posting on social media about it, no public recognition, no telling your friends to get a few pats on the back.

This giving accomplishes two things I particularly like. First of all, you, the giver, get to see the person you're helping. You get to see how they're impacted, and you also get to feel good because you were able to impact their life. Additionally, the recipient can say thanks and know that someone cares and wants to help them.

THE EXCEPTION—EVERYONE KNOWS ABOUT IT

This type of gift does not ultimately meet the criteria for giving without remembering. It's not about getting to say, "Look at me and how generous I've been." It's about doing small—or big—acts of kindness to help others and not looking for recognition. This isn't about you or your status.

However, there's an exception for the "without expectation of return" clause. Only under one circumstance can you tell more people than the recipient. If your purpose is **big enough and you're inspiring others**, then you can break the rules a little.

It's still not about *your* recognition. We're not going out and bragging about the good things we've done. However, if you can create a larger kindness ripple effect by sharing, then it may make sense to do so.

After all, I wrote a book about some of my own good deeds.

Besides, some acts are too big to pull off alone. For example, if you discover a family in need of help, you may need to post on social media—leaving their name off, of course—stating what you're trying to do and rallying other neighbors and friends. This is the exception that allows you to involve others publicly. You *will* get recognition, but you can—and should—downplay your role and play up the role of others, thereby encouraging them to continue to "play" moving forward because they had a positive experience.

Another example comes up all the time for us parents. We're obviously going to involve our kids and show them what we're doing. We want to educate and inspire them.

The key is to make it more about the game and others' participation than your own. Evaluate your intentions carefully before opting for this exception, and you should be fine.

A Few Examples

Here's an example of giving without remembering. Because I gave freely, anonymously, and without expectation of return, I truly didn't remember this act until a few weeks ago when my friend, Christopher, replied to a post on Facebook from a podcast I was on. I didn't remember doing this until he brought it back up, and that's what giving without remembering is all about.

Here is what Christopher wrote:

> "It has been years, my friend, but I'm glad you're doing well. I often talk about the time when—with neither hesitation nor reservation—you offered to lend me (and I accepted) your white Pontiac Fiero because I had no legal transportation at the time. It was an act of kindness that helped me more than I've ever been able to express. I've never forgotten how you acted as though it was no big deal to lend a car for several weeks, but to me it was huge!"

Looking back, I recall having two cars at this point—a red Oldsmobile and a sweet Pontiac Fiero. It wasn't a huge deal for me to lend one out. I doubt I thought about it much when I offered it, but as you can see from the comment Christopher sent me

Rule #1: Give Without Remembering

more than *fifteen years later*, it meant a lot to him, probably for reasons I'll never know. Small act, big difference.

Giving without remembering is a phrase that has been in my head for as long as I can remember. When you give with the pure intention to just help out…that's what I call giving without remembering. You help just to help, and that's that. You're not looking for any recognition.

Freely, anonymously, and without expectation of return.

Keep Your Eyes Open for Opportunities to Play the Game

Here's an interesting element of the goodness game: You don't have to go out actively looking for situations to fix. You can, but you don't *have* to. In this game, we're keeping our eyes open for opportunities that arise where we can help out.

We don't want to force ourselves on anyone.

As an example of how to keep our eyes open, here's a story of James at the bank. He'd come to cash a check and—while waiting in line—overheard a lady with hair as white as snow talking to the teller. The teller said, "If you take out that $20, then you'll only have $96 left in your account."

The white-haired lady replied in a panic, "Are you sure? I need $100 to pay for the hoagie supplies."

By then, James had figured out that this woman was helping with something involving hoagies. A side note: "hoagies" are what people in Pittsburgh call subway sandwiches or subs.

James's heart started racing as he wondered, "Is this an opportunity to act, or am I going to come off as a weirdo?"

Another teller said, "Next."

He deposited his check, got his receipt, and started to leave. Thanks to a later appointment with his tailor—who only took cash—James also had $100 in his pocket. As he walked out of the bank, he spotted the white-haired lady right behind him.

His heart was still racing. It was decision time. He walked to his car, stopped abruptly, and turned to the lady.

"Hello," he said, reaching out with the money from his pocket, "I think you need this more than me."

She started crying and gave James a huge hug. "God bless you!" she said. "You don't know how much this means to me."

He told her, "No problem! I hope you have a great day."

Then he was gone.

This is an example of giving without remembering. He never learned her name, and she never learned his. The opportunity popped up, and—because he was looking—he noticed it, acted, and then he was done.

I'm telling James's story to hopefully inspire you to keep your eyes open so you can do the same thing. Welcome to the goodness game! Maybe you are unable to help the same way James did, and that brings us to Rule # 2!

RULE #2:
IDENTIFY YOUR HELPING STYLE

> "REMEMBER, IF YOU EVER NEED A HELPING HAND, IT'S AT THE END OF YOUR ARM."
>
> —AUDREY HEPBURN

So, you're probably wondering now, "What kind of helper am I?" Finding out your helping style is crucial to playing the goodness game. It's the difference between success and failure. If you don't understand how you can help others effectively, you'll take on challenges you can't complete.

What Kind of Helper am I?

Everyone is different. I want to offer a few examples from people in my personal life who inspire me every day. Hopefully, they'll inspire you with the vastly different ways they're able to help.

Take my mother, for example. She's a special kind of helper. She's laser-focused and super persistent. While not a doctor, she's learned how to deal with the medical system and uses that knowledge to help others. Particularly, she seems to have a superpower for getting people the Disability Social Security they're entitled to. For those who need that assistance, help navigating the system is truly a huge gift.

My brother is a Twitch streamer under the name Dinky Dana. He has a very different style of helping. Thanks to his audience, he's able to carry out fundraising initiatives. He once did a stream to raise money for children with medical issues through an organization called Extra Life. Extra Life is a fundraising program that partners with video game streamers to raise money for children in need. This is his giving style—and he's good at it. He took his skillset and his audience and connected them with Extra Life.

My wife, Tiffany, works with kids. She's patient and understanding at a level I can't quite comprehend, and she loves kids so much that she took a job in an elementary school helping those with special needs. Not many could thrive in this job, but she loves it. That's her helping style.

One more: My mother-in-law, Brenda, gets her friends together every year to pick a family in need. They all pitch in to buy them Christmas gifts. This isn't a huge burden for Brenda and her friends—especially as they combine their funds—but this is certainly a blessing for the family, especially the kids who wouldn't usually have Christmas presents.

You might be objecting right now. "I don't know anything about disability social security," or "I'm not a Twitch streamer" or any number of objections.

That's okay; neither am I! I don't understand medical paperwork, or how to stream on Twitch, or how to help special needs kids. Those aren't my helping styles, and they may not be yours, either.

But guess what? I still help how I can.

Everyone has their own style. There's no wrong way to help. The point is that you need to find YOUR helping style. Take the Helper's Heart Test to see what type of helper you are:

The Five Types of Helpers

I find that many people want to help but don't know how. People underestimate the impact they can make and how little effort it sometimes takes to make a difference.

I had this issue in the past, as well. Here's what I learned: When I help people in the way I was built to help—when I apply my 'helper type'—it becomes so much easier. I feel good, not drained.

What's a 'helper type'?

It's how you play the game. It's your style. The way I see it, you can play one of five ways (though I'm sure there are more ways out there):

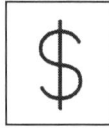

Financial Helper: You prefer—and are able—to help people financially. Basically, you're the "money guy." Don't scoff! Helping with our finances is just as genuine as helping any other way.

Empathetic Helper: You want to help people by paying with your time. I'm not talking about sweat equity—that's next—I'm talking about being there for someone. Listening to them, caring for them, etc.

Sweat Helper: Here we go—the heavy lifters. Someone needs to move that couch, or install that sink, or fix that car. Maybe you have a unique set of skills you like to use, or maybe you just like to get your hands dirty. Sweat Helpers can help people by paying with sweat equity.

Connecting Helper: Maybe you're heavily connected, or maybe you know where to point people who need help. Connecting Helpers can help by connecting people in need with specialized help. You can be the person that "has a guy."

Thinking Helper: You can be the thinker who uses your brain to help people solve their problems. Planning a group project? Looking to organize a fundraiser? Thinking Helpers thrive in these situations.

Rule #2: Identify Your Helping Style

But, how do you know what type of helper you are?

Let's take a look at a scenario to help you determine what type of helper you're built to be. As you read the example below, think about where you'd like to help and what you'd try to avoid. There will be a short quiz after to pull it all together for you.

Helper's Heart Test

Let's say there's an that goes to your city and cares for the homeless every Sunday. This includes things like providing clothing, food, and self-care items/services. To keep their operations running, they'll need help in multiple areas. People will have to:

- Buy the food
- Cook the food
- Hand out the food
- Organize all the volunteers and the event itself
- Donate goods like tents, underwear, socks, and shoes
- Store the donations
- Talk with the homeless to find out what they need
- Solicit donations and volunteers
- Perform self-care for the homeless, like haircuts
- Connect people that need help with specialists who can help them
- Help the homeless remain hopeful

- Organize shelter by finding rentals or connecting people with homeless shelters
- Find a landlord that will accept someone who's living on the streets
- Find/buy furniture for the person moving
- Pick up the furniture and move it
- Help people find jobs
- Help someone get on Disability Social Security if they qualify
- Provide help with medical or health issues
- Map out the entire plan to make sure everyone is where they need to be
- Dealing with the finances, bookkeeping, and volunteers
- Organizing the non-profit
- Creating connections in the community
- Finding ways to raise money

And the list can go on. You can see how many moving parts one small organization can have. Take a look at this list and see what grabs your attention. Do you like to cook? Do you like to connect with people? Are you one of those weird folks who *likes* moving? Whatever catches your eye will probably be the area you're best fit to help. Now that you've read the scenario and thought about your place in it, let's look at your preferences more closely.

You may notice that you fall into more than one helping style. That's normal. The main goal with this exercise is to find

Rule #2: Identify Your Helping Style

out what's NOT your helping style so you know what to avoid. We want to find out what your preferred style is in order to avoid things that are going to drain your energy.

Now, let's look at the example with the homeless organization. We'll separate all the various tasks by helping style to help you decide where you might fit. You may notice the same tasks repeated by different helping styles. That's because it's not always a one-size-fits-all! Different helpers can help in all kinds of ways.

 FINANCIAL HELPER

- Buy the food
- Donate goods like tents, underwear, socks, and shoes
- Find/buy furniture for the person moving

 EMPATHETIC HELPER

- Talk with the homeless to find out what they need
- Organize shelter by finding rentals or connect people with homeless shelters
- Help people find jobs
- Help the homeless remain hopeful

 SWEAT HELPER

- Cook the food
- Hand out the food
- Store the donations
- Pick up the furniture and move it

- Provide help with medical or health issues
- Perform self-care for the homeless, like haircuts

 CONNECTING HELPER

- Solicit donations and volunteers
- Connect people who need help with specialists who can help them
- Help people find jobs
- Find a landlord who will accept someone who's living on the streets
- Help someone get on Disability Social Security if they qualify
- Provide help with medical or health issues
- Create connections in the community

 THINKING HELPER

- Organize all the volunteers and the event itself
- Help someone get on Disability Social Security if they qualify
- Map out the entire plan to make sure everyone is in place
- Deal with the finances, bookkeeping, and volunteers
- Organize the non-profit
- Create connections in the community
- Find ways to raise money

Did you see a few things that resonated with you? I'm sure you felt connected to more than one type of helper. I fall into a few of the categories: The Financial Helper, Connecting Helper, and Thinking Helper. That's where I usually help the most. That's not to say I can't help in other areas—we all can—but I *enjoy* helping in these three.

Make a mental note—or a physical one—on the categories that you jive with. These are the areas where you should focus. Take what you learned above and think on it for a bit. Find what "feels" good, and that's probably your helper style.

The Energy Element

Now that you know what type of helper you are, I want to talk about energy. Not in a spiritual way or anything like that, but I want to talk about it in a way that determines what I believe we're "built" to do. I first heard this from my buddy Trevor Mauch on my podcast, "Eat, Sleep, Invest," when he talked about Dan Martell's energy audit from the book *Buy Back Your Time*.

Here's how it works: We all do things every day. Some of the things we do daily give us energy and some of the things take energy away from us. I'll give you a simple tool to do an energy audit so you can determine some of the things you should be doing more of and some of the things you should do less of. This test has helped me in both my business and personal life, and I think it's relevant here as we're deciding what we want to do while playing the game.

The instructions are simple: Take a piece of paper or an Excel sheet and make two columns. The column on the left should read *Gives Energy* and the column on the right should read *Drains Energy*.

Think about energy like water in a bucket. If you do something that gives you energy, you're adding to your bucket. If you do something that takes energy away from you, you're depleting your bucket. You want to continuously try to add to your bucket so it's overflowing, enabling you to give wholeheartedly. It's hard to give when your bucket is depleted, so you should always be careful when considering activities that deplete you.

Take five minutes per day for a week to write down everything you do. Put them in one of the two columns. The *Gives Energy* column should—hopefully—be a list of the things you enjoy. When you do these things, you should end up with equal or more energy than when you started. The *Drains Energy* column will likely be a list of the things that you do only because you have to. These are the things that you can do—and might even be good at—but when you're done, you feel depleted and tired. For example, if you ask me to clean the house, my energy immediately drops. On the other hand, if you ask me to organize data and create processes—sounds boring, I know—I actually feel my energy rising. Both are boring, both involve organizing things, yet one gives me energy and one drains it.

On the next page, there's an example of my energy audit so you can get an idea of how to set yours up.

Grab a pen and jot down the things that you did today on the blank form on the page following my example. (or, if you prefer not to write in your book, you can find this at www.goodnessgame.com):

Rule #2: Identify Your Helping Style

Energy Audit

the goodness game

Gives Energy	Value	Drains Energy	Value
+ Reading	----	— Cleaning	----
+ Thinking and brainstorming	----	— Cutting the grass	----
+ Making my kids take the trash out	----	— Taking the trash out	----
+ Helping others in one shot	----	— Thinking, not taking action and going round in circles	----
+ Financial donations	----	— Taking on people's burdens	----
+ Public speaking	----	— Small talk	----
+ Doing 1:1's with the team at work	----	— Bookkeeping	----
+ Analyzing marketing data to make decisions	----	— Dealing with insurance and other things like that at work	----
+ Teaching	----	— Paying credit cards and bills (the actual act of doing it)	----
+ Building things	----	— Dealing with legal contracts	----
+ Finding solutions to things	----	— Customer service	----
+ Taking action	----		
+ Solving problems	----		

the goodness game

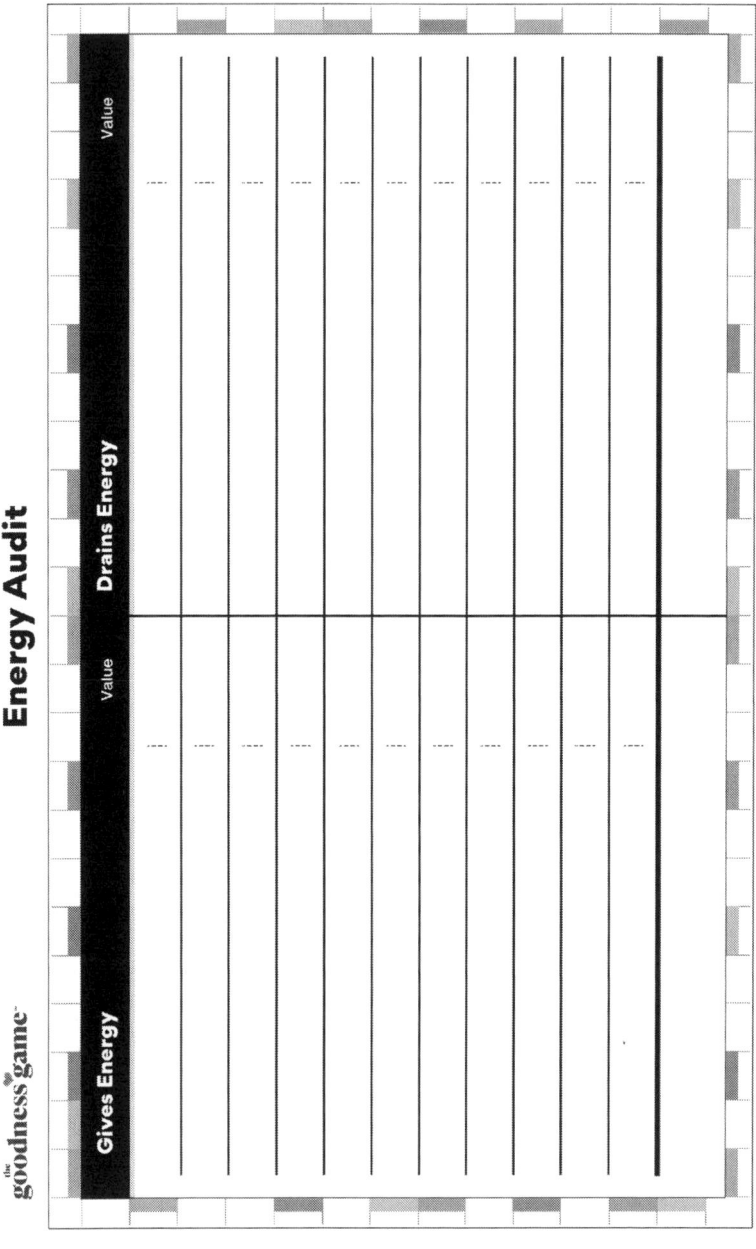

Rule #2: Identify Your Helping Style

Continue adding to your list for the next seven days.

Why am I telling you about energy? Why are we doing this exercise? The purpose of this is to get an idea of the types of things that you should be doing while playing the goodness game.

When you look at my list, you can see I might gravitate toward donating to a cause, sitting down with people trying to accomplish something to brainstorm about their goals, or helping people take action instead of just talking about things. Those are things that are fun for me; they give me energy. Those are things I need to do to keep my bucket full.

Don't get me wrong; those aren't the *only* things I can or should do. If one of my neighbors has an issue and can't cut their grass, I'd do it for them. But that's not going to fill my bucket. I'll be tired after and want to chill out for a bit. You can and should do things that you may not feel optimally inclined to do, but you should also be aware of which things belong in which column so you can make informed decisions when deciding on your strategy for the goodness game. If mowing a lawn is going to make me want to take the rest of the day off, then taking over lawn maintenance for my neighbor on an ongoing basis isn't necessarily going to be productive. However, helping them access ongoing lawn maintenance—or maybe even paying for it myself—is an area I can more easily assist.

My game won't revolve around manual labor, cleaning houses, or dreaming with no action plans. My game revolves around thinking, seeing issues, and taking swift action. Personally, I like to keep my eyes peeled at all times so when I see an issue, I can decide in my head quickly if it's something that's my assignment—more on that in a moment—then act. Once I act, the results often happen quickly. Then I'm done and move back to life. I created and refined this plan after evaluating my energy audit.

What are your top three things that give you energy? What are the top three that drain it? Make a note so you can play the game and crush it with an overflowing bucket!

Sometimes You Need To Accept Help

One final note before we move on to the next rule: It's easy to get so wrapped up in helping others that you forget it's ok to accept help yourself. You may face this pitfall at some point, so it's best to be aware of it from the start.

It's okay to accept help!

By accepting help, you're allowing others to play the game, as well. If you're too proud to accept help, you don't give them the benefit of being able to help. They say it's better to give than to receive, but if we don't receive, then others can't give.

It's important to think about the person offering to help you. Will they benefit or "score"—whether they're officially playing the game or not—by doing this thing for you? Is it something that would legitimately help you out? If the answer to these questions is "Yes," then the right thing to do is accept the help. Don't follow some misguided principle telling you that tough people "go it alone" or some other nonsense. Accept the help and let someone else perform an act of kindness.

It's another win/win.

RULE #3:
NOT EVERYONE IS
YOUR ASSIGNMENT

> "OUR PRIMARY PURPOSE IN THIS LIFE IS TO HELP OTHERS. AND IF YOU CAN'T HELP THEM, AT LEAST DON'T HURT THEM."
>
> – DALAI LAMA

Hopefully, you've got your eyes open now for people to help as you play the goodness game. However, not everyone in the world will be your "assignment." You have to learn to identify areas where you can help and other areas where the only way you can help is by pointing someone to a more qualified individual.

Mike Murdock, author of *The Assignment*, says, "Your assignment on earth is simply the problem God created you to solve."

Whether you're religious or not, the point here is that each of us is built for some things and not built for others—just think about our energy charts from the previous chapter. When playing the game, the goal is to improve the recipient's situation, not to make your situation worse. This isn't a seesaw; we don't want to empty our bucket to fill theirs, because we'll quickly be done helping and our game ends.

The goodness game aims to create win/win situations where both parties are better off than when they started. This can't happen if you consider everyone in need to be your personal assignment. You'll burn out quickly. Also, you're not qualified to assist in every situation. None of us are.

Accepting Help

Don't force your help on people. If you want to help someone, they need to accept your help. Often, when we try to help someone, we want to do it "our way." We need to be aware that our job is to help them and not force anything. Sometimes, this means allowing someone to say "No, thank you," even when we know in our hearts we could assist in a meaningful way. Accepting a "No" is part of making this process about others rather than yourself because if you try to force someone to accept your help, you make the whole thing about you instead of them.

Don't Overstep

The goodness game has rules to keep you safe as well as to protect the hearts and interests of others. Overstepping is a real danger when playing the game. So far I've tried to be pretty sparing with sharing my own charitable ventures—remember rule #1—but this is an opportunity to show a time when helping someone went too far.

I was having a casual discussion with a friend about marketing, telling him, "All you need to do is make sure you have the pixels on your website and make sure the events are firing on the conversion page." Maybe you know those terms, and maybe you don't, but they're related to his Facebook ads. I was trying to explain how to run ads for a group in order to generate more leads. Since we were having a casual talk, I should have left him with a few tips, given him the tools to do things on his own, then stepped back.

But I didn't.

He hadn't asked me to get involved. We were just having a conversation about marketing! In my excitement to help, I said, "You know what? If you want, add me to your Facebook ad account and I'll dive in and take a further look!" My friend agreed, and I was in. I started looking around and saw a few easy things that I believed would improve the efficacy of his marketing. I alerted him, and he thanked me.

Now, at this point, I'd already overstepped a little, though he appreciated the help. It would've been great if I'd stopped there, but once I got access, I couldn't stop looking around. I soon spotted some major problems in his account just glaring at me. The next move I made overstepped my boundaries even more. I wrote him: "Hey, I see a ton wrong in your ad account. If you want, I can rebuild a few of the campaigns and work with your team to help you out."

And there I was, way too involved. How do I get out of this situation? Now we're in a relationship that involves his business and his money, and I'm in the uncomfortable position of sticking my nose in places it doesn't belong.

If he had been a client, things would have been different. In a provider-client relationship, that offer would've been acceptable and fine. But my friend was having a conversation with me and now, probably to his surprise, has found himself in a situation where his buddy has just injected himself into his business and ad account. It felt like quicksand to me, and I expect it did to my friend as well.

When you play the goodness game, it's your responsibility to create whatever boundaries you're comfortable with and be mindful of them. Don't get too excited in the heat of the moment and promise to do things outside your lane.

Make a plan, know your boundaries—and the boundaries of others—and stick to them.

Pitfalls to Avoid as You Play the Goodness Game

Not to be a Debbie Downer, but it's my job at this point. Here's a hard truth: Not everyone can be helped—by you, at least. In some cases, you should help yourself *and* them by stepping away. I don't mean people struggling with mental or physical problems or those dealing with addictions. I mean people who aren't in a place where they're ready to accept assistance. Helping in that situation is a pointless depletion of resources that benefits no one. It's your job to avoid becoming entangled in this sort of relationship.

Ask yourself:

- **Have I helped this person in the past?**
  Maybe you gave them tools in the past, but they didn't use them. Maybe they lied or misled you about how they would use funds you provided. In these cases, you might not actually be helping this person.

- **Do they seem ready to be helped?**
  If you're being asked to make a big effort or sacrifice to help, it can sometimes feel selfish not to do so. However, not all people are ready to accept help. They may misuse or squander your gift. If they're not taking any responsibility for their situation or refusing to help themselves, they may not be ready to accept help from you.

You'll want to be aware of these situations because you need to decide if you can actually help. You need to go with your gut here! Many people genuinely want help but don't want to do what's needed to change their lives.

Tricksters and Schemers

Don't let people mistake kindness for weakness. Beware of tricksters and schemers.

If someone has a drug problem and they come to you for money, ask them what they need the money for. If they say they need it for food, go out and buy them food instead. Or, better yet, take them to the grocery store. If they say they need it for rent, you could pay their landlord directly.

Addictions and mental disorders are tragic. I don't mean to sound like I'm downplaying them; I've suffered from some of these issues myself. It might have been counterproductive if I'd been given money in those times. When your body is under the influence of bad chemicals, you sometimes do bad things. Even though an addict may not intentionally try to hurt you, you must protect yourself in these situations so you don't put yourself in harm's way. You'll also want to be aware of people who want to take advantage of your kindness.

We want to keep our eyes open for opportunities to play the goodness game, but we also need to protect ourselves and not put ourselves in a worse position than we were when we started.

Not everyone is your assignment.

RULE #4: CREATE YOUR GOODNESS BUDGET

> "THE BUDGET IS NOT JUST A COLLECTION OF NUMBERS, BUT THE EXPRESSION OF OUR VALUES AND ASPIRATIONS."
>
> – JACK LEW, AMERICAN ATTORNEY & U.S. AMBASSADOR TO ISRAEL

Years ago, my dad gave me a little yellow book called *The Richest Man in Babylon*. It's an interesting read if you want to get out of debt and be financially free. The book is written in parables, and my favorite section of the book is the "Five Laws of Gold."

The first law of gold is this: "Gold cometh gladly and in increasing quantity to any man who will put by not less than one-tenth his earnings to create an estate for his future and that of his family." In layman's terms, "Save 10% of what you make." It's a pretty solid rule, and it has been around—and working—for literal centuries.

Now, the goodness game isn't a finance book, but hang with me for a minute so I can explain why I'm talking about gold. *The Richest Man in Babylon* was my introduction to creating a budget, and you need a budget for the goodness game—not just a financial one.

When my kids were old enough, I bought one of Dave Ramsey's banks designed especially for kids. If you don't know about them, they're clear and have three sections: Spend, Give, Save.

This was interesting to me. Prior to that, I hadn't thought about creating a budget with funds specifically allocated to "Give." I quickly found that if I had money set aside—and that money was earmarked for giving—it was easy to use that money on giving.

That might seem elementary, but think how many times you might have had good intentions about donating time, money, or energy, and then found yourself unable to fulfill those intentions. We often hear this sort of thing described as "Life got in the way." When you plan ahead, you'll find that life doesn't get in the way so often, and you'll have the budget to give with—whether it's time, money, or energy.

It's easy to get caught up in the hype of helping people and give more than you can afford. One of the biggest stress-related threats you'll encounter as you play the goodness game is burnout. Remind yourself: Too much of anything tends to become a bad thing. If you don't budget and just go wherever you're led by your emotions, you'll risk overexerting and overextending yourself.

I read an article on the Cleveland Clinic's website that said: "Caregiver burnout happens when you devote the majority of your time, energy and resources to taking care of others that you neglect, forget or aren't able to take care of yourself. Not caring for your physical, emotional and mental health can severely impact the way you feel and your ability to complete your personal responsibilities" (Cleveland Clinic 2023).

Let's take a look at how to build our budgets.

Rule #4: Create Your Goodness Budget

Finance Burnout

Think about this. Someone you know has a financial emergency and you want to help, but it's a lot of money. You look at your bank account and debate on helping. You see your money, and maybe you can help, but you'll have to re-work your budget to make room.

It's emotionally challenging. If you're the sort of person who thinks playing the goodness game is a good idea, you also probably want to help everyone as much as possible. This is what I used to do. I used to have to make this kind of difficult decision every time something popped up.

I'd pull the money from my main bank account to help out. Then, I'd see my funds go down and down until I wondered how I'd manage the rest of the month. It was really stressful, and I kept doing it because I believed in my heart—where those darn emotions are—that I was doing the right thing. All the while, I was giving myself financial burnout each time I saw the funds drop.

I did this for years before realizing there was a better way. I wanted to be able to help people out financially without hesitation and without the stress of possibly being strapped for the rest of the month. Finally, I figured out a solution.

I take my income and immediately pull 10% from the top to put in my savings account. This is a reserve account for my family and for me. Next, I pull an additional 10% and put that in the "Give Account." You don't have to pull the same amount—give what you can! This is money that I earmark for situations that pop up in which people need financial help.

Now, when a situation arises and someone needs help, I go into the "Give Account" and pull the money out. There's no thinking involved. The only thinking I have to do is to decide if this is something I want to contribute to. It's not pulling from my monthly living budget; the money in the "Give Account" is there for *this exact reason*.

It takes the emotion out of giving financially.

Time Burnout

If you like helping with your time—or find yourself doing so even if it's not your first choice—you'll want to budget the potential for time burnout into your equation. In the same way we did it for money, we'll do it with time.

Ask yourself, "How much time could I spend weekly to help if opportunities arise?" Really think about it. Don't just pick a number; think about what you could realistically do without maxing your week out or overstressing yourself. Keep in mind

Rule #4: Create Your Goodness Budget

that things will pop up during the week that are out of your control, so you don't want to fill every minute of the day.

Maybe you watch Netflix for an hour a day and scroll on social media for forty-five minutes after work. You might say, "I'm going to budget thirty minutes per day to help out, and I'm going to pull that half hour from my Netflix and social media scrolling."

That might not be you, but the point is to look at your schedule and decide where you can pull the time from—because you're currently spending it doing something—and then budget it for the future. For example, say you have thirty minutes per day that you can budget for the goodness game, and you'll budget this for five days per week. That's two and a half hours per week!

If you stick to your budget, you should be able to avoid time burnout and still get your "points" by playing.

Next, you need to decide how to spend your time. Do you keep it available and wait for something to pop up? Do you sign up for Meals on Wheels and donate thirty minutes daily? Do you budget the entire two and a half hours per week and hook up with an organization that feeds the homeless on Sundays like Harvest Street Mission does?

Time is a cool thing to budget because you can do so many things with it.

You can:
- Feed the homeless
- Clean up trash on the side of the road
- Tutor kids

- Go out and be kind to people for thirty minutes
- Deliver meals to seniors
- Help someone move
- Pick up things for someone because you have a truck
- Connect someone with someone else you know to help both parties

You can do so many more things than just the ones on the list above. Because everyone is different and has a different helping style, you'll have different ideas and know what would work best for you. Be creative! Think about it. Do you have a fun and unique way you helped someone that others can copy? Let us know (anonymously, of course) at www.goodnessgame.com!

The point is: Think ahead so you budget your time so you're not running around like a chicken with its head cut off. Spending time while stressed because you're running out of it isn't very productive, so prepare beforehand.

Energy Burnout

Energy is vital. You'll want to budget for energy based on your energy audit. Determine what type of things you *want* to help with, what things you *can* help with, and what things you *don't* want to help with. Remember your energy bucket; do the things that keep it full!

Pay attention and notice the difference between what you *want* to help with and what you *can* help with. These are crucial. Remember, things you *want* to help with are things that give you energy. These are things you love doing and could do them all day long because you wouldn't get tired or mentally weary while doing them. Things you *can* help with are things that you're good at, but they might not necessarily be things that you enjoy. For example, I can rake my neighbor's leaves in the fall to help out, but I don't enjoy it; it drains my energy.

Lastly, be aware of the things that drain your energy so badly that you don't want to do them. Avoid regularly volunteering to do the things that drain your energy while playing the goodness game. You might have situations where you need to suck it up and help, and that's okay. Just be aware of it ahead of time—*budget* for it.

It's essential to think about your energy and the specific types of things you want and don't want to do ahead of time so that when opportunities arise, you're not making decisions based on emotion and regretting it.

An easy way to do this is to look at your helping style and then match that with things on your energy audit, then you'll have a good idea how to budget.

RULE #5:
KEEPING SCORE!

> **"I SHOOT, I SCORE. HE SHOOTS, I SCORE."**
> – DAN GABLE, ONE OF THE GREATEST WRESTLERS OF ALL TIME

My oldest son has an ongoing debate with his Grandpa. It's pretty simple: which fictional character would win in a fight? Grandpa always chooses Superman. It makes sense; Superman's the strongest superhero out there. Why not always pick him?

In response to Grandpa's somewhat canned challenge, my son will come up with some pretty creative ideas. We go on walks all the time, and on one of these, he was preparing for the next battle with Grandpa and told me his strategy. He'd chosen Mahoraga from Jujutsu Kaisen. Apparently, Mahoraga has massive amounts of strength and speed, but he also has this ability to be immune to anything he gets hit with unless it kills him. Mahoraga once got his head split in half and still lived.

My question to him was, "What's your source?"

Want to know what his answer was?

He said, "Google."

"What?" I replied. "Dude, that's a search engine, not a source."

It's become a thing between the two of us, kind of jokingly and kind of not. I'm always asking him the source of whatever he tells me because I want to make sure he can determine what's true and what's not in this digital world where anyone can post whatever they want online.

Why am I telling you this? Easy: the goodness game works. Unlike my son, I've got *actual* sources that aren't "Google." We already proved the model in action, but here are a few more statistics showing how kindness is a win/win.

Did you know?

Being kind to someone releases feel-good chemicals in our brains that help us feel happier. It's known as a "Helpers High." According to *Explore: The Journal of Science and Healing*, "The concept of the 'helper's high' arose in the 1980s, and has been confirmed in various studies since then. It consists of positive emotions following selfless service to others. Greater health and increased longevity are associated with this psychological state (Dossey 2018)."

According to *Integrative Psychological and Behavior*, perpetually kind people have 23% less cortisol—the stress

Rule #5: Keeping Score!

hormone—and age more slowly than the average population. Kindness boosts our energy levels. A study found that people felt stronger and more energetic after helping others. Kindness has been shown to slow the aging process! It causes the release of oxytocin, which can reduce free radicals and inflammation in our bodies, slowing aging at the source. (McCraty, et al. 1998).

A WebMD articles states that, "Oxytocin is the mediator of what has been called the 'tend-mend' response, as opposed to the 'fight-flight' response to stress. When you're altruistic and touching people in a positive way, lending a helping hand, your oxytocin level goes up—and that relieves your own stress" (Davis n.d.). This happens despite the added stress that sometimes accompanies helping others.

Have you noticed that when you're kind to someone, you feel good inside? Acts of kindness are often accompanied by a feeling of emotional warmth, which in turn produces the hormone oxytocin in your body. Oxytocin causes the release of a chemical called nitric oxide, which expands your blood vessels, reduces blood pressure, and protects your heart (The Science of Kindness, 2022).

With all this information, you can see that if you help others consistently and play with others—just like when I called Sean Martin with the umbrellas—your body and brain chemicals will be affected positively. We can track this data and prove these statistics are true by using our own Scorecards when playing the goodness game.

Let's talk about how to track and prove this.

Your Scorecard

In my marketing business, I'm constantly looking at our ROI—our *return on investment*. What I'm looking for is to see how much return I get for every dollar spent. For example, say I spend $1 on marketing and bring in $2 in sales. I'd consider that a 2X ROI, meaning I spent one dollar and turned it into two. For those of you who like numbers, tracking, and KPIs—key performance indicators—this section is for you. If numbers make your head spin, don't worry. We have a way for you to track as well.

But we're not in business here—we're playing a game. We still need a scorecard right? We're going to track our ROI a little differently. We're going to track it as a Return On Impact (you can find the scorecard on www.goodnessgame.com).

As a reminder, we're not playing against others. This isn't that kind of game. You're playing for yourself *and* others. The scorecard allows us to track our results from how hard something is for us to do (energy), how we feel before and after (inner results), and what our impact is (outside results).

This is important because the scorecard will help you track what "fits" with your energy and helping style. You can track what has the best benefit for you and others and try to adapt and do more of that. You can see what you're doing that might be taking energy away from you and be aware of those things in the future.

As often attributed to Peter Drucker, "What gets measured gets managed."

Rule #5: Keeping Score!

Tracking your results on the scorecard will give you clarity, create consistency, and show you concretely that the small acts you're doing are creating a ripple effect in both you and others.
Tracking your results on the scorecard will give you clarity, create consistency, and show you concretely that the small acts you're doing are creating a ripple effect in both you and others.
You can download your own scorecard at www.goodnessgame.com

.

the goodness game

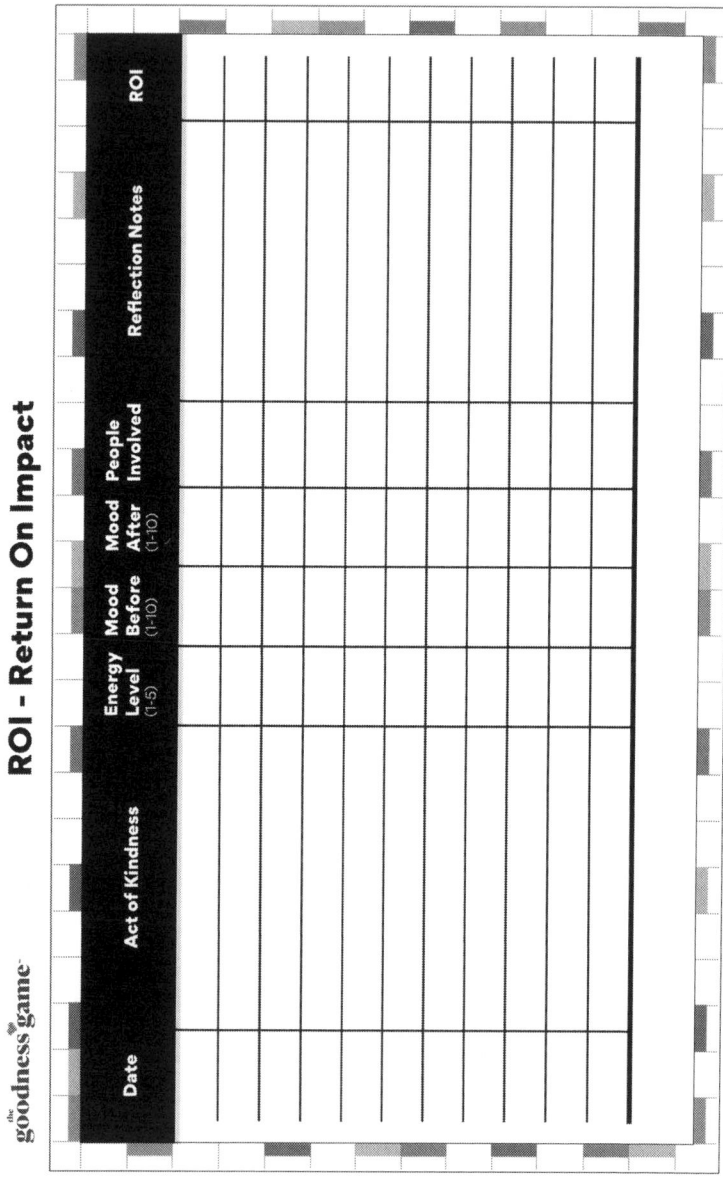

Rule #5: Keeping Score!

The Goodness Journal

For those of you who don't like tracking numbers and charts, I have an alternative. If you journal already, you probably know what to do here and have your style.

For those of you who are new to journaling, I'll give a little guidance to help you get started.

Ask yourself:
- How has your life changed while playing the game?
- What are you experiencing?
- Tell a story of what you did and what happened.
- How did you feel before and after playing the goodness game?
- What are the positive outcomes?
- What reactions are you getting from people that you're helping?
- What life experiences have you had that you wouldn't have otherwise? (Get out of your bubble!)
- What's your #1 reason to keep playing?
- Are you noticing anything changing in your life?
- What ideas popped into your head that were inspired by playing?

It doesn't matter if you use the scorecard, journal, or have an alternative way to track your progress; the main point is to track your progress to see what impact you're having while playing the goodness game. Also, when you're feeling drained, you can see the impact you're having as you play the game, both on your own mental health and on the world around you.

THE COMPOUND EFFECT OR "THE KINDNESS RIPPLE"

> **"NO ACT OF KINDNESS, NO MATTER HOW SMALL, IS EVER WASTED."**
>
> – AESOP

Have you ever helped someone and then just moved on? Like it was a nice thing to do—but you didn't expect anything to come from it except for a nice experience.

It feels good. It's satisfying. You tend to want more.

I think that could be what the lady in Florida felt like. There's no way for me to know how she feels, but I feel certain she does not know the ripple effect she created in my life and others. From her one action, she has helped hundreds more people. The lady picking me up in Florida created a ripple effect that she'll never even know about. She changed the course of my life—and possibly saved it. She made me think differently and inspired me to act to help others. People have been helped in the United States, Guatemala, Canada, Montenegro, and I'm sure other places, all because she picked me up and fed me.

Think about the butterfly effect, the phenomenon by which a small change at one place in a complex system can have large effects elsewhere. By helping me out—a small change at one place—she triggered me to have large effects elsewhere. After all, I've been playing this game for more than twenty years and counting.

I think about this a lot. As humans, we always want to see what happens when we do something. We want to see cause and effect. We want to know we made a difference.

I met my wife through a small, single act of kindness.

Tiffany almost didn't stay in Pittsburgh long enough for us to ever meet. My wife is originally from Ohio and moved to Pittsburgh before meeting me. She always worked two jobs and worked hard. The problem was she was always about $100 behind every month after paying her bills. Finally, in December 2009, she decided that this was a turning point and a sign that she was supposed to move back home to Ohio. She was talking with her mom's friend, Minnie, and telling her about this, and Minnie asked her, "Do you think Pittsburgh is where you are supposed to be?"

Tiffany told her, "Yes, I think this is where I'm supposed to be. It's just every month, I'm struggling and about $100 short."

Minnie told Tiffany, "I'll tell you what: I'll give you $100 this month to help you out, and if it's the place you should be, things will work out for you."

I met my wife a month later, on January 29, 2010!

If you think about this, if Minnie hadn't helped my Tiffany out that month, we wouldn't have met, we wouldn't be married, I wouldn't have three beautiful kids, and our lives would be completely different. All from one person being kind and helping my wife out.

By the way: *Thanks, Minnie!*

Think about your life. Has someone done something that affected your life in a major way? Something small that

The Compound Effect or "The Kindness Ripple"

changed your trajectory? Take a moment to realize that one of the many small things you'll do—or have already done—has a high probability of changing someone's life. It's crazy to think that something as small as $100 has changed how the last twelve years of my life have been.

Sometimes, it's small things that make a huge difference in someone's life. A long time ago, as my dad was giving to a homeless man on the side of the road, I asked him, "What if they just buy drugs or waste the money?"

He told me, "It's not our job to judge. If they're on the side of the road, they're worse off than we are, and it's our job to try to help if we can. Whatever they do with the money is on them. A lot of people will buy drugs, waste it, or use it for no good. Maybe they're not ready to change yet. But for one of those people, it might change their life."

This is also true for the lady who helped me on the side of the road. She was my person, an angel that saved my life. She doesn't know it and will never know all the good that came from it, but she did it for whatever her reasons were, and it changed my life.

I can only assume she thought the same way as my dad.

I think about this when I give to people. I remind myself my job is to give without remembering. I give, and then I imagine. I imagine this could be the time that changes someone's life for the better. Most of the time, it won't be, but it *could* be. And sometimes, it is.

Let's look at this like golf. Pretend you could hit a golf ball as many times as you liked at fifty yards away from the hole, and when you made it in, you'd get $1 million. If you had unlimited shots, do you think one of those shots would get in? It might take fifty shots, it might take five thousand, but one of them will make it in.

I think about it like that. If you consistently keep taking shots, one of them will make a large ripple. Also, on the plus side, every time you take a shot your bucket gets fuller. You feel better after each shot, and your scorecard will prove it—it's a true win/win.

Inspire Others

When you play the goodness game, every time you do good for someone, you inspire new potential players in the game. Say your neighbor just had surgery, and they're down for a week. When you connect with neighbors, friends, and family to start bringing them food daily, you just recruited new players.

By taking the small act to help them and communicating with the "new players," you just played the game. You create new players when you play the game in front of your kids. When you help your friend pack and move, you create new players. Do you think someone is more likely to help a friend move when they've received this kind of help in the past?

Just think about moving. It pretty much sucks. I'm sure you know what I'm talking about. First, you need to decide what to keep and what to get rid of. Then, you spend all day—or longer—packing all your stuff. Finally, you have to move it all.

And refrigerators are heavy!

Most people can't move on their own. So, what do you do? You ask for help.

The Compound Effect or "The Kindness Ripple"

Whenever my friends and family help me move, I'm grateful. Of course, I buy them pizza when we're done to thank them. But let's be honest; they didn't help me move for a "thank you" pizza. Pizza isn't payment. If you asked anyone to move an entire household for a pizza, they'd say no. It's not an even trade.

So, if someone helps you move a refrigerator, they're not doing it for a pizza; they're helping because they care about you. They don't want you to die under a heavy appliance, alone and squished, because they didn't help you. That's something they're doing for *you*. Pizza—which still isn't a payment—is something you do for *them* because you appreciate their assistance and the relationship.

But something else happens here, too. When you're asked to help someone else move in the future, you're more likely to do it because someone helped you. Remember the kindness ripple? You're the ripple now. Someone helped you, so now you want to help someone else, then that person will want to help someone else, and so on.

It's like compound interest. Did you know if you invested $1 and contributed $1 monthly for fifty years, you would have saved $601.00? Congrats! You can retire.

Okay, maybe not.

But if you look beyond just the cash you're investing and assume a modest 7% interest—that's the ripple—you'd end up with $5,062.41.

Quite a difference!

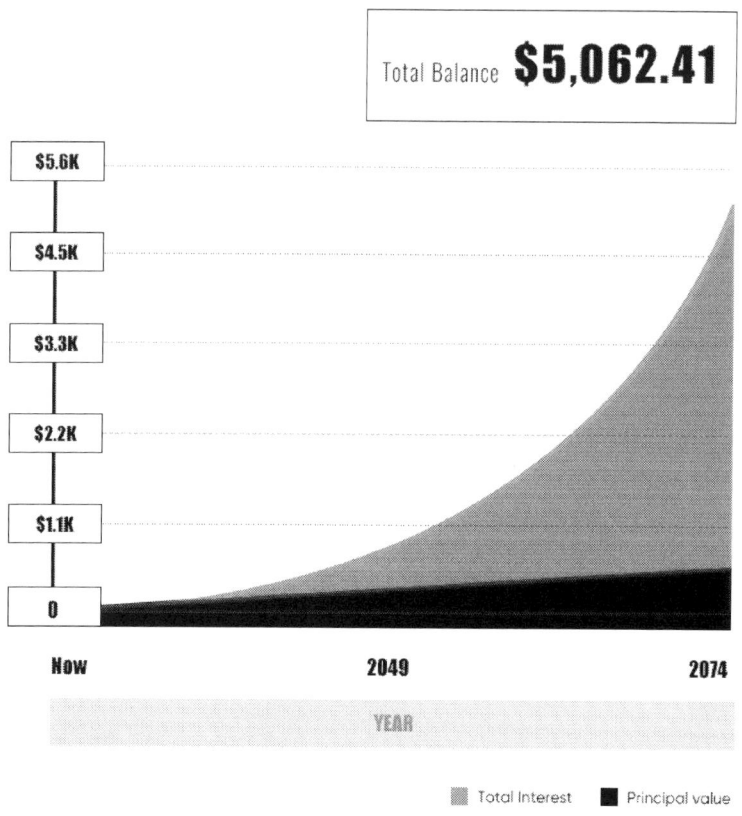

It's easy to see the effect in the image, but the compound effect isn't visible most of the time in the real world. The compounding happens years later. Even in the compound interest example above it took about ten years to see the lines start to split and the compounding happen.

The ripple effect might not always be visible to you. Sometimes, that's the fun part. You get to think, "I wonder who got the underwear and socks that I donated," or, "I wonder what that mom felt like when I donated the beds and mattresses for her kids."

Imagine it like this: You show kindness to person A, which encourages person A to be kind to others and inspires bystander B to follow suit. A's and B's acts of kindness then ripple out, influencing C, D, and beyond. In this way, your kind gesture creates a chain reaction of positivity, directly and indirectly.

In an August 2022 study published by the University of Texas, researchers found that while people who performed "random acts of kindness" tend to underestimate how great a positive effect the act will have, the recipients of these acts tend to remember them far longer than the giver expects—and in a far more positive light. Furthermore, they're more likely to take on the "challenge" of doing acts of kindness themselves in the future. (Science Daily 2022).

"People tend to think that what they are giving is kind of little, maybe relatively inconsequential," explained the lead researcher in a *New York Times* article. She continued, "Recipients are less likely to think along those lines. They consider the gesture to be more meaningful because they are also thinking about the fact that someone did something nice for them" (Pearson 2022).

The Inner Effect—Having Faith in Exponential Growth

Do good things, and good things come. This is where faith comes into play because you can't see the results all the time. The lady that helped me didn't even trigger anything in my brain for years. But when it finally did, it triggered something still alive today.

It's like the Karma Law: Whatever energy and thoughts you put out in the world, you get back. They can either be good or bad, but they're coming back. By playing the game, we're putting out positive energy and also thinking positively—this is what your scorecard should reflect as well with your mood and ROI, your Return on Impact.

You get multiple benefits when you play the game, as well. It's a cool byproduct. You help others, and they get help, while you also get help! It could be Karma. It could be oxytocin. It could be both and more. There are multiple reasons this happens.

The point is that by helping others, you're helping yourself, as well.

Think about it. When you volunteer, do you feel better or worse when you're done? I've almost always felt like I got more out of the experience when I volunteer than the people I'm helping. Remember, it's called the "helper's high," so it makes sense that you'd want to continue doing it.

Why wouldn't you want to do something that helps others and makes you feel better? Try it yourself; if you're having a tough day and don't want to get out of bed, get up and find someone to help. Mark it on your scorecard and see how you feel.

Win/Win

Some people will say if you're helping people to help yourself feel better, then the effort isn't genuine. There's a certain type of person who believes that to be helping "out of the goodness of your heart" you can't also experience benefits from those efforts. They say, "If you intend to feel better yourself, then it's not genuine."

This is something important to talk about. You shouldn't feel guilty because you feel good playing the goodness game. Helping others is helping others. Do you think a person who needs help is really going to mind if you feel better about yourself in the process? No! They want and need the help. If you're incentivized to some degree by the good feeling you get, that works fine for them.

Would I want the guy on the side of the road not to eat tonight because I thought, "This isn't really a genuine act because I'm going to feel better after helping him, so I better not do it."

That would be silly!

During my research for this book, I found some people talking about being "genuine." Their premise was that if you have a motive to help others beyond assisting in its purest form, then what you'd be doing isn't genuine.

What do I have to say about this? Well, let's see: If you're helping someone else, and you feel better, *what's the issue? This seems more like a win/win scenario.*

When you start helping people, you're going to feel better, and you may see and notice things you didn't notice before. You might be more motivated or have a more positive outlook on life. You might be more confident knowing that you have the ability and strength to make a difference in someone else's life. You might be proud of your kids when you see how they want to play the goodness game. You might be closer to your family and friends because you're all doing something for a common goal. You might meet some new people who become friends. You might wake up motivated and roll out of bed with a bounce instead of hitting the alarm clock, dreading the day. You might start imagining things you could do or be more creative.

Science says you're going to feel better due to chemicals in your brain. There are so many ways you could grow internally when you play the goodness game.

It's truly awesome!

The cool thing here is everyone will have a different experience. Everyone is different. They look at the world differently and help people differently, so your experience will be different than mine.

You also don't have to take my word for it. You'll have concrete evidence in your scorecard or your goodness journal showing true cause and effect. You'll be able to see specific actions you took and what happened internally because of those actions.

I know my life has changed immensely since I started playing, and it has changed for the better. I'm constantly looking for times to play the goodness game. I feel good knowing when an opportunity arises, I can act immediately. I know the exact helping situations that I'm cut out for and, more importantly, the ones I'm not. There's so much peace and confidence in knowing that.

The Compound Effect or "The Kindness Ripple"

I'm able to notice others playing the game now. I no longer think the world is as bad as everyone makes it out to be. I pay attention to what I see at the grassroots level. It makes me think that the world isn't all doom and gloom like we see in the media.

When you start playing the goodness game, you might feel as if you've taken off a pair of glasses you forgot were tinted because you've been wearing them for so long. It's kind of like slipping those glasses off and realizing the sky isn't actually as dark and stormy as you thought. I once had a pair of yellow driving glasses because they were supposed to help me drive at night. I tried them on one day, wore them for a few minutes, and then took them off. The world looked completely different. It almost looked like it had a hint of purple to it. It was so beautiful! My eyes had adjusted to the yellow glasses and made everything look "normal" when I was wearing them, and when I took them off, everything looked different.

I notice things like that when playing the goodness game. Playing the game gives you a slightly different look at the world. You see things clearer. Just take a look at your scorecard. The world will look brighter when you look up again.

My point is this: When you help others, you'll also feel good. It's a true **win/win,** *and that's okay.*

So, what are you waiting for?

JUST DO IT!

> **"THE SECRET OF GETTING AHEAD IS GETTING STARTED."**
>
> – MARK TWAIN

You thought we were done? One more tiny chapter—I promise—then you can go and play the goodness game.

I used to get so wrapped up in wanting to know every little detail whenever I planned to start something. I wanted to think and think and make sure nothing could go wrong. But you know what? I'd never really get started on a lot of the things I wanted to do.

I'm sure you can relate. Sometimes, you want to get started but keep thinking of what else you need to know, or you want to think about what could go wrong so you can prepare for it.

Some call this paralysis by analysis. I used to fall for this trap as well.

We're going to do the exact opposite here.

We're going to **start today**!

Like right now!

I can say this because you don't have to think. I've done all the thinking for you.

The steps are easy!

> **Step 1**—Determine what your helper type is.
>
> **Step 2**—Take the energy audit (available at www.goodnessgame.com) to find ways you can help AND not get drained.
>
> **Step 3**—Do something today that fits your helper type and gives you energy.

Super simple.

Remember: It's the small things that make a big difference. You're not looking for some large, overwhelming thing to do in your life. Look for the small, simple things. This will be so small and take so little effort that you'll think, "That was it?"

If you need a few ideas, here are a few to get you started:

- Hold the door open for someone, smile at them, and say, "Hi!"
- Give your waiter/waitress a big tip and write them a note on the back of the receipt saying thanks.
- Talk with your kids about the game and get them to give you their ideas. Kids have awesome ideas because they haven't been punched in the face by the world yet.
- Put some cash in your pocket so the next time you see someone in need you're prepared (I know most people don't carry cash these days).
- Call that family member that you've been feuding with and try to make amends. Cutting out the negative energy there will help both of you.

- Get uncomfortable if necessary and say "okay" to the organization looking for volunteers.
- When you're having a conversation with someone, pay attention and actually listen when they're talking. I know a lot of the time when I'm talking with someone, I'm thinking about what I'm going to say as soon as they're done speaking. Slow down and listen. They'll notice, I promise.

Just do something!

Here's the thing: It's like a snowball rolling down a hill. All you need to do is give it that slight push, and it starts moving. It'll gain momentum and take you where you need to go.

You now have the roadmap to making a difference in the world, probably bigger than you could imagine. Small acts can make a big difference. The goodness game is like dominoes: one good deed leads to another, and another, and another.

So, let's recap the goodness game:

Give Without Remembering: Try to help people blindly without bragging.

Identify Your Helping Style - Stay in your lane, which you now know because you took the Helper's Heart Test and energy audit.

Not Everyone is Your Assignment: Don't try to help everyone.

Create Your Goodness Budget: Budget your time, energy, and money. No one does well if they burn out.

Push the Snowball Down the Hill: The compound effect is real. By playing the goodness game, you will be doing small acts that will compound quickly.

Feel Good: Get ready to see a difference in your life. Karma is real, and you're about to experience it in a positive way.

And most importantly…

Take Action and start playing the goodness game!

BIBLIOGRAPHY

2023. *Cleveland Clinic.* August 16. https://my.clevelandclinic.org/health/diseases/9225-caregiver-burnout.

Davis, Jeanie Lerche. n.d. *The Science of Good Deeds.* Accessed September 18, 2024. https://www.webmd.com/balance/features/science-good-deeds.

Dossey, Larry. 2018. *ScienceDirect.* November. Accessed September 18, 2024. https://www.sciencedirect.com/science/article/abs/pii/S1550830718304178?via%3Dihub.

McCraty, R, B Barrios-Choplin, D Rozman, M Atkinson, and A D Watkins. 1998. "National Library of Medicine." *Integrative Psychological and Behavioral Science* 151-70. https://pubmed.ncbi.nlm.nih.gov/9737736/.

Pearson, Catherine. 2022. September 2. https://www.nytimes.com/2022/09/02/well/family/random-acts-of-kindness.html.

2022. *School of Kindness.* https://schoolofkindness.org/wp-content/uploads/2022/02/School-Of-Kindness-Printable-Posters.pdf.

2022. *Science Daily.* August 18. https://www.sciencedaily.com/releases/2022/08/220818164056.htm.

2022. *The Science of Kindness.* https://schoolofkindness.org/wp-content/uploads/2022/01/Science-of-Kindness-Download.pdf.

Wolf, Jessica. 2023. *Is Kindness Contagious.* January 5. https://newsroom.ucla.edu/magazine/bedari-kindness-institute-contagious.

ABOUT THE AUTHOR

Bryan Driscoll is a first-time author with a passion for inspiring kindness and creating positive change in the world. Twenty years ago, a stranger literally picked him up off the street and gave him a plate of spaghetti and a bedroom he had to share with an oversized cat. This small act of kindness sparked an unending desire to pay it forward, ultimately leading to *the goodness game*.

He lives in Pittsburgh (*go Steelers!*) with an amazing wife who puts up with his insanity—and probably encourages it more than she should. He has three sons, all different and awesome in their own way. They say they get their awesomeness from their father, and he won't argue, even if everyone knows the truth.

He runs a successful digital marketing agency and is an active real estate investor, though he'd tell you his biggest strength is getting back up when life punches him in the face. And it's punched him quite a few times, though a few of those punches might have been deserved.

When he's not working, Bryan enjoys mountain biking, skiing with his sons, and spending time with his family. He focuses on living in the moment, avoiding the distractions of social media, and helping others achieve personal and professional growth through public speaking and teaching.

Made in the USA
Middletown, DE
27 November 2024

65267638R00068